CAT ON A HOT TIN ROOF

BY TENNESSEE WILLIAMS

PLAYS

Baby Doll & Tiger Tail
Camino Real
Candles to the Sun
Cat on a Hot Tin Roof
Clothes for a Summer Hotel
Fugitive Kind
The Glass Menagerie
A House Not Meant to Stand
A Lovely Sunday for Creve Coeur
Mister Paradise and Other One Act Plays
Not About Nightingales
The Notebook of Trigorin
Something Cloudy, Something Clear
Spring Storm
Stairs to the Roof
Stopped Rocking and Other Screen Plays
A Streetcar Named Desire
Sweet Bird of Youth
27 Wagons Full of Cotton and Other Plays
The Traveling Companion and Other Plays
The Two-Character Play
Vieux Carré

THE THEATRE OF TENNESSEE WILLIAMS, VOLUME I
Battle of Angels, A Streetcar Named Desire, The Glass Menagerie
THE THEATRE OF TENNESSEE WILLIAMS, VOLUME II
The Eccentricities of a Nightingale, Summer and Smoke,
The Rose Tattoo, Camino Real
THE THEATRE OF TENNESSEE WILLIAMS, VOLUME III
Cat on a Hot Tin Roof, Orpheus Descending, Suddenly Last Summer
THE THEATRE OF TENNESSEE WILLIAMS, VOLUME IV
Sweet Bird of Youth, Period of Adjustment, The Night of the Iguana
THE THEATRE OF TENNESSEE WILLIAMS, VOLUME V
The Milk Train Doesn't Stop Here Anymore, Kingdom of Earth
(The Seven Descents of Myrtle), Small Craft Warnings, The Two-Character Play
THE THEATRE OF TENNESSEE WILLIAMS, VOLUME VI
27 Wagons Full of Cotton and Other Short Plays
THE THEATRE OF TENNESSEE WILLIAMS, VOLUME VII
In the Bar of a Tokyo Hotel and Other Plays
THE THEATRE OF TENNESSEE WILLIAMS, VOLUME VIII
Vieux Carré, A Lovely Sunday for Creve Coeur, Clothes for a Summer Hotel,
The Red Devil Battery Sign

POETRY

Collected Poems
In the Winter of Cities

PROSE

Collected Stories
Hard Candy and Other Stories
One Arm and Other Stories
Memoirs
The Roman Spring of Mrs. Stone
The Selected Letters of Tennessee Williams, Volume I
The Selected Letters of Tennessee Williams, Volume II
Where I Live: Selected Essays

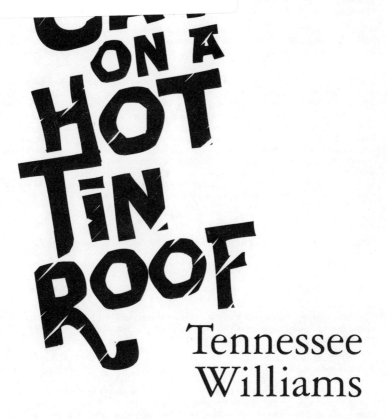

CAT ON A HOT TIN ROOF

Tennessee Williams

with an Introduction by EDWARD ALBEE

A NEW DIRECTIONS BOOK

The editor thanks Mitch Douglas for his continued support and for generously sharing his extensive knowledge about Tennessee Williams.

The Dylan Thomas epigraph is from "Do not Go Gentle into that Good Night," from *The Selected Poems of Dylan Thomas, 1934-1952*, copyright 1952 by Dylan Thomas, published by New Directions.

Design by Semadar Megged
Manufactured in the United States of America
New Directions Books are printed on acid-free paper.
First published clothbound by New Directions in 1955. This revised version of the play, first published clothbound and as New Directions Paperbook 398 in 1975. Reissued with an Introduction by Edward Albee as New Directions Paperbook 997 in 2004.
Published simultaneously in Canada by Penguin Canada Books, Ltd.

Library of Congress Cataloging-in-Publication Data

Williams, Tennessee, 1911-1983.
  Cat on a hot tin roof / by Tennessee Williams.
    p. cm.
  ISBN 978-0-8112-1601-2 (alk. paper)
  1. Inheritance and succession--Drama. 2. Fathers and sons--Drama. 3. Terminally ill--Drama.
4. Mississippi--Drama. I. Title.
  PS3545.I5365C37 2004
  812'.54--dc22   2004011665

Fifth Printing

New Directions Books are published for James Laughlin
by New Directions Publishing Corporation
80 Eighth Avenue, New York 10011

CONTENTS

Introduction by Edward Albee   7

Production credits   12

Notes for the Designer   15

Cat on a Hot Tin Roof   17

"Swinging a Cat" by Brian Parker   175

"Author and Director: A Delicate Situation"
by Tennessee Williams   187

Chronology   193

INTRODUCTION

by Edward Albee

There's this very funny story about George Bernard Shaw—and I hope it's true!—that when he was nicely into his nineties he would reread one of his plays, or perhaps see a production, and have trouble following what was happening. These complexities—the story goes—troubled him for, to his mind, they indicated that the plays were too complex—too recondite, perhaps—for proper absorption and that he'd best simplify them: better late than never.

It did not occur to Shaw that the problem was with him and not the plays, and his publishers had to take the work away from him before he reduced them all to a fodder suitable to someone in their first or second childhood.

Someone wrote that a creative work is never finished but abandoned, and the suggestion is cautionary, even if not intended so. Scholars and interviewers ask me frequently whether I will go back to a play years after I've finished (or, abandoned) it—revise, rethink.

I tell them no, explaining that the person who wrote *The American Dream*, say, back in 1959, is not exactly the same person 40-some years later, that the errors (be they such) in that play are the enthusiasms of youth, and that while a sober reexamining may make one cringe a bit at the excesses (again, be they such) these two "people" are not, while friendly, in useful contact.

Take *The Zoo Story*, of 1958, as a case. The only changes I have allowed myself in that play are the bringing of a few specifics up to date—dollar values for example, or the identity of "popular" writers of the time. This is a play which is set "in the present" and must not have anachronisms.

As well, I could not resist the temptation to trim back an aria-like moment in the play: Jerry is dying, a knife buried deep in his belly, probably slicing the aorta. He then delivers a half page of rather good stuff, but I took a knife of my own to it and brought it down to a proper two sentences.

I did the same thing to an eleven-minute aria in *Tiny Alice* which John Gielgud objected to back in 1962 when I was sure that every word I wrote was both sacrosanct and properly so. Time and craft taught me that John Gielgud was right, and if he would like to do the play again, in heaven or wherever, he will have a far more playable third act.

I'm certain that if I were to reread one of my plays from years ago and decide I no longer subscribed to its premises, I would either withdraw it from performance or, more likely, just let it sit as it is. I certainly would not rewrite it.

I doubt I will have the George Bernard Shaw problem as my plays are fairly simple and I imagine I will still comprehend them when I reach great age.

Tennessee Williams' *Cat On A Hot Tin Roof* is almost as famous for its revisions as it is for its final text. Knowing that Tennessee was well known for tinkering with his plays, often long after he wrote them, and that he was overly fond of just about anyone's advice during the rehearsal process, I am not surprised that there are several texts of *Cat On A Hot Tin Roof*; the play Tennessee wrote in 1955, the version Elia Kazan persuaded him to do for the Broadway production of that same year, and the so-called "solution" in which Tennessee kept some of Kazan's "improvements" and rejected others. Most of Kazan's ideas were good ones—made the play more structurally sound and dramatically "forward moving." Some—the ones

Williams rejected ultimately—were a little "commercial," an attempt to make the play...well, more commercial. Kazan could be as crass as the next man and he was always as interested in his own career as he was in anyone else's.

It's a fine play—especially in its final version—and if one can quarrel with some of its operatic gestures, and if a few of its characters seem smaller than life, or perhaps more rudimentary, Williams' accomplishment is, as it is in all of his best work, highly romantic and tough at the same time, its prose capable of elevated flights yet remaining tethered to reality and—more importantly—believability.

Tennessee Williams was a romantic poet of the theatre—much like Lorca—yet the driving force was less metaphor than actuality. His plays read beautifully and—in accurate performances—play beautifully as well.

The pressure on playwrights to revise their work for production—more often than not to the detriment of the work—deserves an essay of its own. Suffice it to say here that commercial pressures to render plays toothless (and thereby pointless) are growing as the economies of the theatre become more crippling. The back and forth between Kazan and Williams was innocent play by comparison. Besides, many of Kazan's ideas (especially the reemergence of Big Daddy in the last act) were helpful to the dramatic coherence of the play, and Tennessee's reinstatement of the irony and ambiguity in the final moments of the play was an equally wise one.

I'm sorry Kazan moved exclusively to film work before he and I had the possibility of working together. Considering all I know of his creative relationships with Tennessee Williams and Arthur Miller I am certain I would have enjoyed the push and pull.

New York City, 2004

9

for Maria

Cat on a Hot Tin Roof was originally presented at the Morosco Theatre in New York on March 24, 1955 starring Barbara Bel Geddes, Ben Gazzara, Mildred Dunnock and Burl Ives, directed by Elia Kazan. That version of the play and its variant third act are published in New Directions' *Theatre of Tennessee Williams, Volume III*.

On July 10, 1974 *Cat on a Hot Tin Roof* was restaged by the American Shakespeare Theatre in Stratford, Connecticut, with the third act rewritten, along with other substantial revisions. That version of the play, which is printed here, reopened in New York on September 24, 1974 at the ANTA Theatre. Both 1974 productions were directed by Michael Kahn; designed by John Conklin, with lighting by Marc B. Weiss, and costumes by Jane Greenwood. The cast was as follows:

MARGARET	Elizabeth Ashley
BRICK	Keir Dullea
DIXIE, a little girl	Deborah Grove
MAE, sometimes called Sister Woman	Joan Pape
GOOPER, sometimes called Brother Man	Charles Siebert
BIG MAMA	Kate Reid
SOOKEY, a Negro servant	Saraellen

BIG DADDY	Fred Gwyne
REVEREND TOOKER	Wyman Pendleton
DOCTOR BAUGH, pronounced "Baw"	William Larsen
LACEY, a Negro servant*	Thomas Anderson
CHILDREN*	Jeb Brown, Chris Browning Betsy Spivak Susannah Brown

*In the New York production, the part of Lacey was not included, and the number of children was reduced to three, played by Jeb Brown, Sukie Brown and Amy Borress.

And you, my father, there on the sad height,
Curse, bless, me now with your fierce tears, I pray.
Do not go gentle into that good night.
Rage, rage against the dying of the light.

Dylan Thomas

NOTES FOR THE DESIGNER

The set is the bed-sitting-room of a plantation home in the Mississippi Delta. It is along an upstairs gallery which probably runs around the entire house; it has two pairs of very wide doors opening onto the gallery, showing white balustrades against a fair summer sky that fades into dusk and night during the course of the play, which occupies precisely the time of its performance, excepting, of course, the fifteen minutes of intermission.

Perhaps the style of the room is not what you would expect in the home of the Delta's biggest cotton-planter. It is Victorian with a touch of the Far East. It hasn't changed much since it was occupied by the original owners of the place, Jack Straw and Peter Ochello, a pair of old bachelors who shared this room all their lives together. In other words, the room must evoke some ghosts; it is gently and poetically haunted by a relationship that must have involved a tenderness which was uncommon. This may be irrelevant or unnecessary, but I once saw a reproduction of a faded photograph of the verandah of Robert Louis Stevenson's home on that Samoan Island where he spent his last years, and there was a quality of tender light on weathered wood, such as porch furniture made of bamboo and wicker, exposed to tropical suns and tropical rains, which came to mind when I thought about the set for this play, bringing also to mind the grace and comfort of light, the reassurance it gives, on a late and fair afternoon in summer, the way that no matter what, even dread of death, is gently touched and soothed by it. For the set is the background for a play that deals with human extremities of emotion, and it needs that softness behind it.

The bathroom door, showing only pale-blue tile and silver towel racks, is in one side wall; the hall door in the opposite wall. Two articles of furniture need mention: a big double bed which staging should make a functional part of the set as often as suitable, the surface of which should be slightly raked to make figures on it seen more easily; and against the wall space between the two huge double doors upstage: a monumental monstrosity peculiar to our times, a *huge* console combination of radio-phonograph (hi-fi with three speakers) TV set *and* liquor cabinet, bearing and containing many glasses and bottles, all in one piece, which is a composition of muted silver tones, and the opalescent tones of reflecting glass, a chromatic link, this thing, between the sepia (tawny gold) tones of the interior and the cool (white and blue) tones of the gallery and sky. This piece of furniture (?!), this monument, is a very complete and compact little shrine to virtually all the comforts and illusions behind which we hide from such things as the characters in the play are faced with. . . .

The set should be far less realistic than I have so far implied in this description of it. I think the walls below the ceiling should dissolve mysteriously into air; the set should be roofed by the sky; stars and moon suggested by traces of milky pallor, as if they were observed through a telescope lens out of focus.

Anything else I can think of? Oh, yes, fanlights (transoms shaped like an open glass fan) above all the doors in the set, with panes of blue and amber, and above all, the designer should take as many pains to give the actors room to move about freely (to show their restlessness, their passion for breaking out) as if it were a set for a ballet.

An evening in summer. The action is continuous, with two intermissions.

16

ACT ONE

At the rise of the curtain someone is taking a shower in the bathroom, the door of which is half open. A pretty young woman, with anxious lines in her face, enters the bedroom and crosses to the bathroom door.

MARGARET [*shouting above roar of water*]:
One of those no-neck monsters hit me with a hot buttered biscuit so I have t' change!

[*Margaret's voice is both rapid and drawling. In her long speeches she has the vocal tricks of a priest delivering a liturgical chant, the lines are almost sung, always continuing a little beyond her breath so she has to gasp for another. Sometimes she intersperses the lines with a little wordless singing, such as "Da-da-daaaa!"*]

[*Water turns off and Brick calls out to her, but is still unseen. A tone of politely feigned interest, masking indifference, or worse, is characteristic of his speech with Margaret.*]

BRICK:
Wha'd you say, Maggie? Water was on s' loud I couldn't hearya. . . .

MARGARET:
Well, I!—just remarked that!—one of th' no-neck monsters messed up m' lovely lace dress so I got t'—cha-a-ange. . . .

[*She opens and kicks shut drawers of the dresser.*]

BRICK:
Why d'ya call Gooper's kiddies no-neck monsters?

MARGARET:
Because they've got no necks! Isn't that a good enough reason?

17

BRICK:
Don't they have any necks?

MARGARET:
None visible. Their fat little heads are set on their fat little bodies without a bit of connection.

BRICK:
That's too bad.

MARGARET:
Yes, it's too bad because you can't wring their necks if they've got no necks to wring! Isn't that right, honey?

[*She steps out of her dress, stands in a slip of ivory satin and lace.*]

Yep, they're no-neck monsters, all no-neck people are monsters . . .

[*Children shriek downstairs.*]

Hear them? Hear them screaming? I don't know where their voice boxes are located since they don't have necks. I tell you I got so nervous at that table tonight I thought I would throw back my head and utter a scream you could hear across the Arkansas border an' parts of Louisiana an' Tennessee. I said to your charming sister-in-law, Mae, honey, couldn't you feed those precious little things at a separate table with an oilcloth cover? They make such a mess an' the lace cloth looks *so* pretty! She made enormous eyes at me and said, "Ohhh, noooooo! On Big Daddy's birthday? Why, he would never forgive me!" Well, I want you to know, Big Daddy hadn't been at the table two minutes with those five no-neck monsters slobbering and drooling over their food before he threw down his fork an' shouted, "Fo' God's sake, Gooper, why don't you put them pigs at a trough in th' kitchen?"—Well, I swear, I simply could have di-ieed!

Think of it, Brick, they've got five of them and number six is coming. They've brought the whole bunch down here like animals to display at a county fair. Why, they have those children doin' tricks all the time! "Junior, show Big Daddy how you do this, show Big Daddy how you do that, say your little piece fo' Big Daddy, Sister. Show your dimples, Sugar. Brother, show Big Daddy how you stand on your head!"—It goes on all the time, along with constant little remarks and innuendos about the fact that you and I have not produced any children, are totally childless and therefore totally useless! —Of course it's comical but it's also disgusting since it's so obvious what they're up to!

BRICK [*without interest*]:
What are they up to, Maggie?

MARGARET:
Why, you know what they're up to!

BRICK [*appearing*]:
No, I don't know what they're up to.

[*He stands there in the bathroom doorway drying his hair with a towel and hanging onto the towel rack because one ankle is broken, plastered and bound. He is still slim and firm as a boy. His liquor hasn't started tearing him down outside. He has the additional charm of that cool air of detachment that people have who have given up the struggle. But now and then, when disturbed, something flashes behind it, like lightning in a fair sky, which shows that at some deeper level he is far from peaceful. Perhaps in a stronger light he would show some signs of deliques-*

19

cence, but the fading, still warm, light from the gallery treats him gently.]

MARGARET:
I'll tell you what they're up to, boy of mine!—They're up to cutting you out of your father's estate, and—

[She freezes momentarily before her next remark. Her voice drops as if it were somehow a personally embarassing admission.]

—Now we know that Big Daddy's dyin' of—cancer. . . .

[There are voices on the lawn below: long-drawn calls across distance. Margaret raises her lovely bare arms and powders her armpits with a light sigh.

[She adjusts the angle of a magnifying mirror to straighten an eyelash, then rises fretfully saying:]

There's so much light in the room it—

BRICK [softly but sharply]:
Do we?

MARGARET:
Do we what?

BRICK:
Know Big Daddy's dyin' of cancer?

MARGARET:
Got the report today.

BRICK:
Oh . . .

MARGARET [letting down bamboo blinds which cast long, gold-fretted shadows over the room]:

Yep, got th' report just now . . . it didn't surprise me, Baby.
. . .

[*Her voice has range, and music; sometimes it drops low as a boy's and you have a sudden image of her playing boy's games as a child.*]

I recognized the symptoms soon's we got here last spring and I'm willin' to bet you that Brother Man and his wife were pretty sure of it, too. That more than likely explains why their usual summer migration to the coolness of the Great Smokies was passed up this summer in favor of—hustlin' down here ev'ry whipstitch with their whole screamin' tribe! And why so many allusions have been made to Rainbow Hill lately. You know what Rainbow Hill is? Place that's famous for treatin' alcoholics an dope fiends in the movies!

BRICK:
I'm not in the movies.

MARGARET:
No, and you don't take dope. Otherwise you're a perfect candidate for Rainbow Hill, Baby, and that's where they aim to ship you—over my dead body! Yep, over my dead body they'll ship you there, but nothing would please them better. Then Brother Man could get a-hold of the purse strings and dole out remittances to us, maybe get power of attorney and sign checks for us and cut off our credit wherever, whenever he wanted! Son-of-a-bitch!—How'd you like that, Baby?— Well, you've been doin' just about ev'rything in your power to bring it about, you've just been doin' ev'rything you can think of to aid and abet them in this scheme of theirs! Quittin' work, devoting yourself to the occupation of drinkin'! —Breakin' your ankle last night on the high school athletic field: doin' what? Jumpin' hurdles? At two or three in the

21

morning? Just fantastic! Got in the paper. *Clarksdale Register* carried a nice little item about it, human interest story about a well-known former athlete stagin' a one-man track meet on the Glorious Hill High School athletic field last night, but was slightly out of condition and didn't clear the first hurdle! Brother Man Gooper claims he exercised his influence t' keep it from goin' out over AP or UP or every goddam "P."

But, Brick? You still have one big advantage!

[*During the above swift flood of words, Brick has reclined with contrapuntal leisure on the snowy surface of the bed and has rolled over carefully on his side or belly.*]

BRICK [*wryly*]:
Did you *say* something, Maggie?

MARGARET:
Big Daddy dotes on you, honey. And he can't stand Brother Man and Brother Man's wife, that monster of fertility, Mae. Know how I know? By little expressions that flicker over his face when that woman is holding fo'th on one of her choice topics such as—how she refused twilight sleep!—when the twins were delivered! Because she feels motherhood's an experience that a woman ought to experience fully!—in order to fully appreciate the wonder and beauty of it! HAH!—and how she made Brother Man come in an' stand beside her in the delivery room so he would not miss out on the "wonder and beauty" of it either!—producin' those no-neck monsters. . . .

[*A speech of this kind would be antipathetic from almost anybody but Margaret; she makes it oddly funny, because her eyes constantly twinkle and her voice shakes with laughter which is basically indulgent.*]

—Big Daddy shares my attitude toward those two! As for

me, well—I give him a laugh now and then and he tolerates me. In fact!—I sometimes suspect that Big Daddy harbors a little unconscious "lech" fo' me. . . .

BRICK:
What makes you think that Big Daddy has a lech for you, Maggie?

MARGARET:
Way he always drops his eyes down my body when I'm talkin' to him, drops his eyes to my boobs an' licks his old chops! Ha ha!

BRICK:
That kind of talk is disgusting.

MARGARET:
Did anyone ever tell you that you're an ass-aching Puritan, Brick?

I think it's mighty fine that that ole fellow, on the doorstep of death, still takes in my shape with what I think is deserved appreciation!

And you wanta know something else? Big Daddy didn't know how many little Maes and Goopers had been produced! "How many kids have you got?" he asked at the table, just like Brother Man and his wife were new acquaintances to him! Big Mama said he was jokin', but that ole boy wasn't jokin', Lord, no!

And when they infawmed him that they had five already and were turning out number six!—the news seemed to come as a sort of unpleasant surprise . . .

[*Children yell below.*]

Scream, monsters!

[Turns to Brick with a sudden, gay, charming smile which fades as she notices that he is not looking at her but into fading gold space with a troubled expression.

[It is constant rejection that makes her humor "bitchy."]

Yes, you should of been at that supper-table, Baby.

[Whenever she calls him "baby" the word is a soft caress.]

Y'know, Big Daddy, bless his ole sweet soul, he's the dearest ole thing in the world, but he does hunch over his food as if he preferred not to notice anything else. Well, Mae an' Gooper were side by side at the table, direckly across from Big Daddy, watchin' his face like hawks while they jawed an' jabbered about the cuteness an' brillance of th' no-neck monsters!

[She giggles with a hand fluttering at her throat and her breast and her long throat arched.

[She comes downstage and recreates the scene with voice and gesture.]

And the no-neck monsters were ranged around the table, some in high chairs and some on th' *Books of Knowledge,* all in fancy little paper caps in honor of Big Daddy's birthday, and all through dinner, well, I want you to know that Brother Man an' his partner never once, for one moment, stopped exchanging pokes an' pinches an' kicks an' signs an' signals! —Why, they were like a couple of cardsharps fleecing a sucker.—Even Big Mama, bless her ole sweet soul, she isn't th' quickest an' brightest thing in the world, she finally noticed, at last, an' said to Gooper, "Gooper, what are you an' Mae makin' all these signs at each other about?"—I swear t' goodness, I nearly choked on my chicken!

[Margaret, back at the dressing table, still doesn't see

24

Brick. He is watching her with a look that is not quite definable —Amused? shocked? contemptuous?—part of those and part of something else.]

Y'know—your brother Gooper still cherishes the illusion he took a giant step up on the social ladder when he married Miss Mae Flynn of the Memphis Flynns.

But I have a piece of Spanish news for Gooper. The Flynns never had a thing in this world but money and they lost that, they were nothing at all but fairly successful climbers. Of course, Mae Flynn came out in Memphis eight years before I made my debut in Nashville, but I had friends at Ward-Belmont who came from Memphis and they used to come to see me and I used to go to see them for Christmas and spring vacations, and so I know who rates an' who doesn't rate in Memphis society. Why, y'know ole Papa Flynn, he barely escaped doing time in the Federal pen for shady manipulations on th' stock market when his chain stores crashed, and as for Mae having been a cotton carnival queen, as they remind us so often, lest we forget, well, that's one honor that I don't envy her for!—Sit on a brass throne on a tacky float an' ride down Main Street, smilin', bowin', and blowin' kisses to all the trash on the street—

[*She picks out a pair of jeweled sandals and rushes to the dressing table.*]

Why, year before last, when Susan McPheeters was singled out fo' that honor, y' know what happened to her? Y'know what happened to poor little Susie McPheeters?

BRICK [*absently*]:
No. What happened to little Susie McPheeters?

MARGARET:
Somebody spit tobacco juice in her face.

BRICK [*dreamily*]:
Somebody spit tobacco juice in her face?

MARGARET:
That's right, some old drunk leaned out of a window in the
Hotel Gayoso and yelled, "Hey, Queen, hey, hey, there,
Queenie!" Poor Susie looked up and flashed him a radiant
smile and he shot out a squirt of tobacco juice right in poor
Susie's face.

BRICK:
Well, what d'you know about that.

MARGARET [*gaily*]:
What do I know about it? I was there, I saw it!

BRICK [*absently*]:
Must have been kind of funny.

MARGARET:
Susie didn't think so. Had hysterics. Screamed like a banshee.
They had to stop th' parade an' remove her from her throne
an' go on with—

[*She catches sight of him in the mirror, gasps slightly,
wheels about to face him. Count ten.*]

—Why are you looking at me like that?

BRICK [*whistling softly, now*]:
Like what, Maggie?

MARGARET [*intensely, fearfully*]:
The way y' were lookin' at me just now, befo' I caught your
eye in the mirror and you started t' whistle! I don't know how
t' describe it but it froze my blood!—I've caught you lookin'
at me like that so often lately. What are you thinkin' of
when you look at me like that?

BRICK:
I wasn't conscious of lookin' at you, Maggie.

MARGARET:
Well, I was conscious of it! What were you thinkin'?

BRICK:
I don't remember thinking of anything, Maggie.

MARGARET:
Don't you think I know that—? Don't you—?—Think I
know that—?

BRICK [*coolly*]:
Know *what*, Maggie?

MARGARET [*struggling for expression*]:
That I've gone through this—*hideous!*—*transformation*, become—*hard! Frantic!*

[*Then she adds, almost tenderly:*]

—*cruel!!*

That's what you've been observing in me lately. How could
y' help but observe it? That's all right. I'm not—thin-skinned
any more, can't afford t' be thin-skinned any more.

[*She is now recovering her power.*]

—But Brick? Brick?

BRICK:
Did you say something?

MARGARET:
I was *goin' t'* say something: that I get—lonely. Very!

BRICK:
Ev'rybody gets that . . .

27

MARGARET:
Living with someone you love can be lonelier—than living entirely *alone*!—if the one that y' love doesn't love you. . . .

[*There is a pause. Brick hobbles downstage and asks, without looking at her:*]

BRICK:
Would you like to live alone, Maggie?

[*Another pause: then—after she has caught a quick, hurt breath:*]

MARGARET:
No!—God!—I wouldn't!

[*Another gasping breath. She forcibly controls what must have been an impulse to cry out. We see her deliberately, very forcibly, going all the way back to the world in which you can talk about ordinary matters.*]

Did you have a nice shower?

BRICK:
Uh-huh.

MARGARET:
Was the water cool?

BRICK:
No.

MARGARET:
But it made y' feel fresh, huh?

BRICK:
Fresher. . . .

MARGARET:
I know something would make y' feel *much* fresher!

BRICK:
What?

MARGARET:
An alcohol rub. Or cologne, a rub with cologne!

BRICK:
That's good after a workout but I haven't been workin' out, Maggie.

MARGARET:
You've kept in good shape, though.

BRICK [*indifferently*]:
You think so, Maggie?

MARGARET:
I always thought drinkin' men lost their looks, but I was plainly mistaken.

BRICK [*wryly*]:
Why; thanks, Maggie.

MARGARET:
You're the only drinkin' man I know that it never seems t' put fat on.

BRICK:
I'm gettin' softer, Maggie.

MARGARET:
Well, sooner or later it's bound to soften you up. It was just beginning to soften up Skipper when—

[*She stops short.*]

I'm sorry. I never could keep my fingers off a sore—I wish you *would* lose your looks. If you did it would make the martyrdom of Saint Maggie a little more bearable. But no such goddam luck. I actually believe you've gotten better looking since you've gone on the bottle. Yeah, a person who didn't

29

know you would think you'd never had a tense nerve in your body or a strained muscle.

[*There are sounds of croquet on the lawn below: the click of mallets, light voices, near and distant.*]

Of course, you always had that detached quality as if you were playing a game without much concern over whether you won or lost, and now that you've lost the game, not lost but just quit playing, you have that rare sort of charm that usually only happens in very old or hopelessly sick people, the charm of the defeated.—You look so cool, so cool, so enviably cool.

REVEREND TOOKER [*off stage right*]:
Now looka here, boy, lemme show you how to get outa that!

MARGARET:
They're playing croquet. The moon has appeared and it's white, just beginning to turn a little bit yellow. . . .

You were a wonderful lover. . . .

Such a wonderful person to go to bed with, and I think mostly because you were really indifferent to it. Isn't that right? Never had any anxiety about it, did it naturally, easily, slowly, with absolute confidence and perfect calm, more like opening a door for a lady or seating her at a table than giving expression to any longing for her. Your indifference made you wonderful at lovemaking—*strange?*—but true. . . .

REVEREND TOOKER:
Oh! That's a beauty.

DOCTOR BAUGH:
Yeah. I got you boxed.

MARGARET:
You know, if I thought you would never, never, *never* make love to me again—I would go downstairs to the kitchen and

pick out the longest and sharpest knife I could find and stick it straight into my heart, I swear that I would!

REVEREND TOOKER:
Watch out, you're gonna miss it.

DOCTOR BAUGH:
You just don't know me, boy!

MARGARET:
But one thing I don't have is the charm of the defeated, my hat is still in the ring, and I am determined to win!

[*There is the sound of croquet mallets hitting croquet balls.*]

REVEREND TOOKER:
Mmm—You're too slippery for me.

MARGARET:
—What is the victory of a cat on a hot tin roof?—I wish I knew. . . .

Just staying on it, I guess, as long as she can. . . .

DOCTOR BAUGH:
Jus' like an eel, boy, jus' like an eel!

[*More croquet sounds.*]

MARGARET:
Later tonight I'm going to tell you I love you an' maybe by that time you'll be drunk enough to believe me. Yes, they're playing croquet. . . .

Big Daddy is dying of cancer. . . .

What were you thinking of when I caught you looking at me like that? Were you thinking of Skipper?

[*Brick takes up his crutch, rises.*]

Oh, excuse me, forgive me, but laws of silence don't work!
No, laws of silence don't work. . . .

[*Brick crosses to the bar, takes a quick drink, and rubs his
head with a towel.*]

Laws of silence don't work. . . .

When something is festering in your memory or your imagination, laws of silence don't work, it's just like shutting a
door and locking it on a house on fire in hope of forgetting
that the house is burning. But not facing a fire doesn't put it
out. Silence about a thing just magnifies it. It grows and
festers in silence, becomes malignant. . . .

[*He drops his crutch.*]

BRICK:
Give me my crutch.

[*He has stopped rubbing his hair dry but still stands
hanging onto the towel rack in a white towel-cloth robe.*]

MARGARET:
Lean on me.

BRICK:
No, just give me my crutch.

MARGARET:
Lean on my shoulder.

BRICK:
I don't want to lean on your shoulder, I want my crutch!

[*This is spoken like sudden lightning.*]

Are you going to give me my crutch or do I have to get down
on my knees on the floor and—

32

MARGARET:
Here, here, take it, take it!

[*She has thrust the crutch at him.*]

BRICK [*hobbling out*]:
Thanks . . .

MARGARET:
We mustn't scream at each other, the walls in this house have ears. . . .

[*He hobbles directly to liquor cabinet to get a new drink.*]

—but that's the first time I've heard you raise your voice in a long time, Brick. A crack in the wall?—Of composure?

—I think that's a good sign. . . .

A sign of nerves in a player on the defensive!

[*Brick turns and smiles at her coolly over his fresh drink.*]

BRICK:
It just hasn't happened yet, Maggie.

MARGARET:
What?

BRICK:
The click I get in my head when I've had enough of this stuff to make me peaceful. . . .

Will you do me a favor?

MARGARET:
Maybe I will. What favor?

BRICK:
Just, just keep your voice down!

33

MARGARET [*in a hoarse whisper*]:
I'll do you that favor, I'll speak in a whisper, if not shut up completely, if *you* will do *me* a favor and make that drink your last one till after the party.

BRICK:
What party?

MARGARET:
Big Daddy's birthday party.

BRICK:
Is this Big Daddy's birthday?

MARGARET:
You know this is Big Daddy's birthday!

BRICK:
No, I don't, I forgot it.

MARGARET:
Well, I remembered it for you. . . .

[*They are both speaking as breathlessly as a pair of kids after a fight, drawing deep exhausted breaths and looking at each other with faraway eyes, shaking and panting together as if they had broken apart from a violent struggle.*]

BRICK:
Good for you, Maggie.

MARGARET:
You just have to scribble a few lines on this card.

BRICK:
You scribble something, Maggie.

MARGARET:
It's got to be your handwriting; it's your present, I've given him my present; it's got to be your handwriting!

[*The tension between them is building again, the voices becoming shrill once more.*]

BRICK:
I didn't get him a present.

MARGARET:
I got one for you.

BRICK:
All right. You write the card, then.

MARGARET:
And have him know you didn't remember his birthday?

BRICK:
I didn't remember his birthday.

MARGARET:
You don't have to prove you didn't!

BRICK:
I don't want to fool him about it.

MARGARET:
Just write "Love, Brick!" for God's—

BRICK:
No.

MARGARET:
You've *got* to!

BRICK:
I don't have to do anything I don't want to do. You keep forgetting the conditions on which I agreed to stay on living with you.

MARGARET [*out before she knows it*]:
I'm not living with you. We occupy the same cage.

BRICK:
You've got to remember the conditions agreed on.

SONNY [*off stage*]:
Mommy, give it to me. I had it first.

MAE:
Hush.

MARGARET:
They're impossible conditions!

BRICK:
Then why don't you—?

SONNY:
I want it, I want it!

MAE:
Get away!

MARGARET:
HUSH! Who is out there? Is somebody at the door?

[*There are footsteps in hall.*]

MAE [*outside*]:
May I enter a moment?

MARGARET:
Oh, *you!* Sure. Come in, Mae.

[*Mae enters bearing aloft the bow of a young lady's archery set.*]

MAE:
Brick, is this thing yours?

MARGARET:
Why, Sister Woman—that's my Diana Trophy. Won it at the intercollegiate archery contest on the Ole Miss campus.

36

MAE:
It's a mighty dangerous thing to leave exposed round a house full of nawmal rid-blooded children attracted t'weapons.

MARGARET:
"Nawmal rid-blooded children attracted t'weapons" ought t'be taught to keep their hands off things that don't belong to them.

MAE:
Maggie, honey, if you had children of your own you'd know how funny that is. Will you please lock this up and put the key out of reach?

MARGARET:
Sister Woman, nobody is plotting the destruction of your kiddies. —Brick and I still have our special archers' license. We're goin' deer-huntin' on Moon Lake as soon as the season starts. I love to run with dogs through chilly woods, run, run leap over obstructions—

[*She goes into the closet carrying the bow.*]

MAE:
How's the injured ankle, Brick?

BRICK:
Doesn't hurt. Just itches.

MAE:
Oh, my! Brick—Brick, you should've been downstairs after supper! Kiddies put on a show. Polly played the piano, Buster an' Sonny drums, an' then they turned out the lights an' Dixie an' Trixie puhfawmed a toe dance in fairy costume with *spahkluhs!* Big Daddy just beamed! He just beamed!

MARGARET [*from the closet with a sharp laugh*]:
Oh, I bet. It breaks my heart that we missed it!

[*She reenters.*]

But Mae? Why did y'give dawgs' names to all your kiddies?

MAE:
Dogs' names?

MARGARET [*sweetly*]:
Dixie, Trixie, Buster, Sonny, Polly!—Sounds like four dogs and a parrot . . .

MAE:
Maggie?

[*Margaret turns with a smile.*]

Why are you so catty?

MARGARET:
Cause I'm a cat! But why can't *you* take a joke, Sister Woman?

MAE:
Nothin' pleases me more than a joke that's funny. You know the real names of our kiddies. Buster's real name is Robert. Sonny's real name is Saunders. Trixie's real name is Marlene and Dixie's—

[*Gooper downstairs calls for her. "Hey, Mae! Sister Woman, intermission is over!"—She rushes to door, saying:*]

Intermission is over! See ya later!

MARGARET:
I wonder what Dixie's real name is?

BRICK:
Maggie, being catty doesn't help things any . . .

MARGARET:

I know! *WHY!*—Am I so catty?—Cause I'm consumed with
envy an' eaten up with longing?—Brick, I'm going to lay out
your beautiful Shantung silk suit from Rome and one of your
monogrammed silk shirts. I'll put your cuff links in it, those
lovely star sapphires I get you to wear so rarely. . . .

BRICK:

I can't get trousers on over this plaster cast.

MARGARET:

Yes, you can, I'll help you.

BRICK:

I'm not going to get dressed, Maggie.

MARGARET:

Will you just put on a pair of white silk pajamas?

BRICK:

Yes, I'll do that, Maggie.

MARGARET:

Thank you, thank you so *much!*

BRICK:

Don't mention it.

MARGARET:

Oh, Brick! How long does it have t' go on? This punishment?
Haven't I done time enough, haven't I served my term, can't I
apply for a—pardon?

BRICK:

Maggie, you're spoiling my liquor. Lately your voice always
sounds like you'd been running upstairs to warn somebody
that the house was on fire!

39

MARGARET:
Well, no wonder, no wonder. Y'know what I feel like, Brick?

I feel all the time like a cat on a hot tin roof!

BRICK:
Then jump off the roof, jump off it, cats can jump off roofs and land on their four feet uninjured!

MARGARET:
Oh, yes!

BRICK:
Do it!—fo' God's sake, do it . . .

MARGARET:
Do what?

BRICK:
Take a lover!

MARGARET:
I can't see a man but you! Even with my eyes closed, I just see you! Why don't you get ugly, Brick, why don't you please get fat or ugly or something so I could stand it?

[She rushes to hall door, opens it, listens.]

The concert is still going on! Bravo, no-necks, bravo!

[She slams and locks door fiercely.]

BRICK:
What did you lock the door for?

MARGARET:
To give us a little privacy for a while.

BRICK:
You know better, Maggie.

MARGARET:
No, I don't know better. . . .

[*She rushes to gallery doors, draws the rose-silk drapes across them.*]

BRICK:
Don't make a fool of yourself.

MARGARET:
I don't mind makin' a fool of myself over you!

BRICK:
I mind, Maggie. I feel embarrassed for you.

MARGARET:
Feel embarrassed! But don't continue my torture. I can't live on and on under these circumstances.

BRICK:
You agreed to—

MARGARET:
I know but—

BRICK:
—Accept that condition!

MARGARET:
I CAN'T! CAN'T! CAN'T!

[*She seizes his shoulder.*]

BRICK:
Let go!

[*He breaks away from her and seizes the small boudoir chair and raises it like a lion-tamer facing a big circus cat.*

[*Count five. She stares at him with her fist pressed to her mouth, then bursts into shrill, almost hysterical laughter. He remains grave for a moment, then grins and puts the chair down.*

[*Big Mama calls through closed door.*]

BIG MAMA:
Son? Son? Son?

BRICK:
What is it, Big Mama?

BIG MAMA [*outside*]:
Oh, son! We got the most wonderful news about Big Daddy. I just had t' run up an' tell you right this—

[*She rattles the knob.*]

—What's this door doin', locked, faw? You all think there's robbers in the house?

MARGARET:
Big Mama, Brick is dressin', he's not dressed yet.

BIG MAMA:
That's all right, it won't be the first time I've seen Brick not dressed. Come on, open this door!

[*Margaret, with a grimace, goes to unlock and open the hall door, as Brick hobbles rapidly to the bathroom and kicks the door shut. Big Mama has disappeared from the hall.*]

MARGARET:
Big Mama?

[*Big Mama appears through the opposite gallery doors behind Margaret, huffing and puffing like an old bulldog. She is a short, stout woman; her sixty years and 170 pounds*]

42

have left her somewhat breathless most of the time; she's
always tensed like a boxer, or rather, a Japanese wrestler.
Her "family" was maybe a little superior to Big Daddy's,
but not much. She wears a black or silver lace dress and at
least half a million in flashy gems. She is very sincere.]

BIG MAMA [*loudly, startling Margaret*]:
Here—I come through Gooper's and Mae's gall'ry door.
Where's Brick? *Brick*—Hurry on out of there, son, I just have
a second and want to give you the news about Big Daddy.—
I hate locked doors in a house. . . .

MARGARET [*with affected lightness*]:
I've noticed you do, Big Mama, but people have got to have
some moments of privacy, don't they?

BIG MAMA:
No, ma'am, not in *my* house. [*without pause*] Whacha took
off you' dress faw? I thought that little lace dress was so sweet
on yuh, honey.

MARGARET:
I thought it looked sweet on me, too, but one of m' cute little
table-partners used it for a napkin so—!

BIG MAMA [*picking up stockings on floor*]:
What?

MARGARET:
You know, Big Mama, Mae and Gooper's so touchy about
those children—thanks, Big Mama . . .

[*Big Mama has thrust the picked-up stockings in Margaret's hand with a grunt.*]

—that you just don't dare to suggest there's any room for
improvement in their—

BIG MAMA:
Brick, hurry out!—Shoot, Maggie, you just don't like children.

MARGARET:
I do SO like children! Adore them!—well brought up!

BIG MAMA [gentle—loving]:
Well, why don't you have some and bring them up well, then, instead of all the time pickin' on Gooper's an' Mae's?

GOOPER [shouting up the stairs]:
Hey, hey, Big Mama, Betsy an' Hugh got to go, waitin' t' tell yuh g'by!

BIG MAMA:
Tell 'em to hold their hawses, I'll be right down in a jiffy!

GOOPER:
Yes ma'am!

[She turns to the bathroom door and calls out.]

BIG MAMA:
Son? Can you hear me in there?

[There is a muffled answer.]

We just got the full report from the laboratory at the Ochsner Clinic, completely negative, son, ev'rything negative, right on down the line! Nothin' a-tall's wrong with him but some little functional thing called a spastic colon. Can you hear me, son?

MARGARET:
He can hear you, Big Mama.

BIG MAMA:
Then why don't he say something? God Almighty, a piece of

news like that should make him shout. It made *me* shout, I can tell you. I shouted and sobbed and fell right down on my knees!—Look!

[*She pulls up her skirt.*]

See the bruises where I hit my kneecaps? Took both doctors to haul me back on my feet!

[*She laughs—she always laughs like hell at herself.*]

Big Daddy was furious with me! But ain't that wonderful news?

[*Facing bathroom again, she continues:*]

After all the anxiety we been through to git a report like that on Big Daddy's birthday? Big Daddy tried to hide how much of a load that news took off his mind, but didn't fool *me*. He was mighty close to crying about it *himself!*

[*Goodbyes are shouted downstairs, and she rushes to door.*]

GOOPER:
Big Mama!

BIG MAMA:
Hold those people down there, don't let them go!—Now, git dressed, we're all comin' up to this room fo' Big Daddy's birthday party because of your ankle.—How's his ankle, Maggie?

MARGARET:
Well, he broke it, Big Mama.

BIG MAMA:
I know he broke it.

[*A phone is ringing in hall. A Negro voice answers: "Mistuh Polly's res'dence."*]

I mean does it hurt him much still.

MARGARET:
I'm afraid I can't give you that information, Big Mama.
You'll have to ask Brick if it hurts much still or not.

SOOKEY [*in the hall*]:
It's Memphis, Mizz Polly, it's Miss Sally in Memphis.

BIG MAMA:
Awright, Sookey.

[*Big Mama rushes into the hall and is heard shouting on the phone:*]

Hello, Miss Sally. How are you, Miss Sally?—Yes, well, I
was just gonna call you about it. *Shoot!—*

MARGARET:
Brick, don't!

[*Big Mama raises her voice to a bellow.*]

BIG MAMA:
*Miss Sally? Don't ever call me from the Gayoso Lobby, too
much talk goes on in that hotel lobby, no wonder you can't
hear me!* Now listen, Miss Sally. They's nothin' serious wrong
with Big Daddy. We got the report just now, they's nothin'
wrong but a thing called a—spastic! *SPASTIC!—*colon . . .

[*She appears at the hall door and calls to Margaret.*]

—Maggie, come out here and talk to that fool on the phone.
I'm shouted breathless!

MARGARET [*goes out and is heard sweetly at phone*]:
Miss Sally? This is Brick's wife, Maggie. So nice to hear your
voice. Can you hear *mine?* Well, *good!—*Big Mama just
wanted you to know that they've got the report from the

Ochsner Clinic and what Big Daddy has is a spastic colon.
Yes. Spastic colon, Miss Sally. That's right, spastic colon.
G'bye, Miss Sally, hope I'll see you real soon!

[*Hangs up a little before Miss Sally was probably ready to
terminate the talk. She returns through the hall door.*]

She heard me perfectly. I've discovered with deaf people the
thing to do is not shout at them but just enunciate clearly. My
rich old Aunt Cornelia was deaf as the dead but I could make
her hear me just by sayin' each word slowly, distinctly, close
to her ear. I read her the *Commercial Appeal* ev'ry night, read
her the classified ads in it, even, she never missed a word of it.
But was she a mean ole thing! Know what I got when she
died? Her unexpired subscriptions to five magazines and the
Book-of-the-Month Club and a LIBRARY full of ev'ry dull
book ever written! All else went to her hellcat of a sister . . .
meaner than she was, even!

[*Big Mama has been straightening things up in the room
during this speech.*]

BIG MAMA [*closing closet door on discarded clothes*]:
Miss Sally sure is a case! Big Daddy says she's always got her
hand out fo' something. He's not mistaken. That poor ole
thing always has her hand out fo' somethin'. I don't think
Big Daddy gives her as much as he should.

GOOPER:
Big Mama! Come on now! Betsy and Hugh can't wait no
longer!

BIG MAMA [*shouting*]:
I'm comin'!

[*She starts out. At the hall door, turns and jerks a fore-
finger, first toward the bathroom door, then toward the
liquor cabinet, meaning: "Has Brick been drinking?" Mar-*

garet pretends not to understand, cocks her head and raises her brows as if the pantomimic performance was completely mystifying to her.

[*Big Mama rushes back to Margaret:*]

Shoot! Stop playin' so dumb!—I mean has he been drinkin' that stuff much yet?

MARGARET [*with a little laugh*]:
Oh! I think he had a highball after supper.

BIG MAMA:
Don't laugh about it!—Some single men stop drinkin' when they git married and others start! Brick never touched liquor before he—!

MARGARET [*crying out*]:
THAT'S NOT FAIR!

BIG MAMA:
Fair or not fair I want to ask you a question, one question: D'you make Brick happy in bed?

MARGARET:
Why don't you ask if he makes *me* happy in bed?

BIG MAMA:
Because I know that—

MARGARET:
It works both ways!

BIG MAMA:
Something's not right! You're childless and my son drinks!

GOOPER:
Come on, Big Mama!

[*Gooper has called her downstairs and she has rushed to*

48

the door on the line above. She turns at the door and points at the bed.]

—When a marriage goes on the rocks, the rocks are *there,* right *there!*

MARGARET:
That's—

[*Big Mama has swept out of the room and slammed the door.*]

—not—*fair . . .*

[*Margaret is alone, completely alone, and she feels it. She draws in, hunches her shoulders, raises her arms with fists clenched, shuts her eyes tight as a child about to be stabbed with a vaccination needle. When she opens her eyes again, what she sees is the long oval mirror and she rushes straight to it, stares into it with a grimace and says: "Who are you?"—Then she crouches a little and answers herself in a different voice which is high, thin, mocking: "I am Maggie the Cat!"—Straightens quickly as bathroom door opens a little and Bricks calls out to her.*]

BRICK:
Has Big Mama gone?

MARGARET:
She's gone.

[*He opens the bathroom door and hobbles out, with his liquor glass now empty, straight to the liquor cabinet. He is whistling softly. Margaret's head pivots on her long, slender throat to watch him.*

[*She raises a hand uncertainly to the base of her throat, as if it was difficult for her to swallow, before she speaks:*]

49

You know, our sex life didn't just peter out in the usual way, it was cut off short, long before the natural time for it to, and it's going to revive again, just as sudden as that. I'm confident of it. That's what I'm keeping myself attractive for. For the time when you'll see me again like other men see me. Yes, like other men see me. They still see me, Brick, and they like what they see. Uh-huh. Some of them would give their—

Look, Brick!

[*She stands before the long oval mirror, touches her breast and then her hips with her two hands.*]

How high my body stays on me!—Nothing has fallen on me —not a fraction. . . .

[*Her voice is soft and trembling: a pleading child's. At this moment as he turns to glance at her—a look which is like a player passing a ball to another player, third down and goal to go—she has to capture the audience in a grip so tight that she can hold it till the first intermission without any lapse of attention.*]

Other men still want me. My face looks strained, sometimes, but I've kept my figure as well as you've kept yours, and men admire it. I still turn heads on the street. Why, last week in Memphis everywhere that I went men's eyes burned holes in my clothes, at the country club and in restaurants and department stores, there wasn't a man I met or walked by that didn't just eat me up with his eyes and turn around when I passed him and look back at me. Why, at Alice's party for her New York cousins, the best-lookin' man in the crowd—followed me upstairs and tried to force his way in the powder room with me, followed me to the door and tried to force his way in!

BRICK:
Why didn't you let him, Maggie?

MARGARET:

Because I'm not that common, for one thing. Not that I wasn't almost tempted to. You like to know who it was? It was Sonny Boy Maxwell, that's who!

BRICK:

Oh, yeah, Sonny Boy Maxwell, he was a good end-runner but had a little injury to his back and had to quit.

MARGARET:

He has no injury now and has no wife and still has a lech for me!

BRICK:

I see no reason to lock him out of a powder room in that case.

MARGARET:

And have someone catch me at it? I'm not that stupid. Oh, I might sometime cheat on you with someone, since you're so insultingly eager to have me do it!—But if I do, you can be damned sure it will be in a place and a time where no one but me and the man could possibly know. Because I'm not going to give you any excuse to divorce me for being unfaithful or anything else. . . .

BRICK:

Maggie, I wouldn't divorce you for being unfaithful or anything else. Don't you know that? Hell. I'd be relieved to know that you'd found yourself a lover.

MARGARET:

Well, I'm taking no chances. No, I'd rather stay on this hot tin roof.

BRICK:

A hot tin roof's 'n uncomfo'table place t' stay on. . . .

[*He starts to whistle softly.*]

MARGARET [*through his whistle*]:
Yeah, but I can stay on it just as long as I have to.

BRICK:
You could leave me, Maggie.

[*He resumes whistle. She wheels about to glare at him.*]

MARGARET:
Don't want to and will not! Besides if I did, you don't have
a cent to pay for it but what you get from Big Daddy and he's
dying of cancer!

[*For the first time a realization of Big Daddy's doom seems
to penetrate to Brick's consciousness, visibly, and he looks
at Margaret.*]

BRICK:
Big Mama just said he *wasn't,* that the report was okay.

MARGARET:
That's what she thinks because she got the same story that
they gave Big Daddy. And was just as taken in by it as he
was, poor ole things. . . .

But tonight they're going to tell her the truth about it. When
Big Daddy goes to bed, they're going to tell her that he is
dying of cancer.

[*She slams the dresser drawer.*]

—It's malignant and it's terminal.

BRICK:
Does Big Daddy know it?

MARGARET:
Hell, do they *ever* know it? Nobody says, "You're dying."
You have to fool them. They have to fool *themselves.*

BRICK:
Why?

MARGARET:
Why? Because human beings dream of life everlasting, that's the reason! But most of them want it on earth and not in heaven.

[*He gives a short, hard laugh at her touch of humor.*]

Well. . . . [*She touches up her mascara.*] That's how it is, anyhow. . . . [*She looks about.*] Where did I put down my cigarette? Don't want to burn up the home-place, at least not with Mae and Gooper and their five monsters in it!

[*She has found it and sucks at it greedily. Blows out smoke and continues:*]

So this is Big Daddy's last birthday. And Mae and Gooper, they know it, oh, *they* know it, all right. They got the first information from the Ochsner Clinic. That's why they rushed down here with their no-neck monsters. Because. Do you know something? Big Daddy's made no will? Big Daddy's never made out any will in his life, and so this campaign's afoot to impress him, forcibly as possible, with the fact that you drink and I've borne no children!

[*He continues to stare at her a moment, then mutters something sharp but not audible and hobbles rather rapidly out onto the long gallery in the fading, much faded, gold light.*]

MARGARET [*continuing her liturgical chant*]:
Y'know, I'm *fond* of Big Daddy, I am genuinely fond of that old man, I really *am*, you know. . . .

BRICK [*faintly, vaguely*]:
Yes, I know you are. . . .

MARGARET:

I've always sort of admired him in spite of his coarseness, his four-letter words and so forth. Because Big Daddy *is* what he *is*, and he makes no bones about it. He hasn't turned gentleman farmer, he's still a Mississippi redneck, as much of a redneck as he must have been when he was just overseer here on the old Jack Straw and Peter Ochello place. But he got hold of it an' built it into th' biggest an' finest plantation in the Delta.—I've always *liked* Big Daddy....

[*She crosses to the proscenium.*]

Well, this is Big Daddy's last birthday. I'm sorry about it. But I'm facing the facts. It takes money to take care of a drinker and that's the office that I've been elected to lately.

BRICK:

You don't have to take care of me.

MARGARET:

Yes, I do. Two people in the same boat have got to take care of each other. At least you want money to buy more Echo Spring when this supply is exhausted, or will you be satisfied with a ten-cent beer?

Mae an' Gooper are plannin' to freeze us out of Big Daddy's estate because you drink and I'm childless. But we can defeat that plan. We're *going* to defeat that plan!

Brick, y'know, I've been so God damn disgustingly poor all my life!—That's the *truth,* Brick!

BRICK:

I'm not sayin' it isn't.

MARGARET:

Always had to suck up to people I couldn't stand because they had money and I was poor as Job's turkey. You don't

54

know what that's like. Well, I'll tell you, it's like you would feel a thousand miles away from Echo Spring!—And had to get back to it on that broken ankle . . . without a crutch!

That's how it feels to be as poor as Job's turkey and have to suck up to relatives that you hated because they had money and all you had was a bunch of hand-me-down clothes and a few old moldly three-per-cent government bonds. My daddy loved his liquor, he fell in love with his liquor the way you've fallen in love with Echo Spring!—And my poor Mama, having to maintain some semblance of social position, to keep appearances up, on an income of one hundred and fifty dollars a month on those old government bonds!

When I came out, the year that I made my debut, I had just two evening dresses! One Mother made me from a pattern in *Vogue,* the other a hand-me-down from a snotty rich cousin I hated!

—The dress that I married you in was my grandmother's weddin' gown. . . .

So that's why I'm like a cat on a hot tin roof!

[*Brick is still on the gallery. Someone below calls up to him in a warm Negro voice, "Hiya, Mistuh Brick, how yuh feelin'?" Brick raises his liquor glass as if that answered the question.*]

MARGARET:
You can be young without money, but you can't be old without it. You've got to be old *with* money because to be old without it is just too awful, you've got to be one or the other, either *young* or *with money,* you can't be old and *without* it.—That's the *truth,* Brick. . . .

[*Brick whistles softly, vaguely.*]

55

Well, now I'm dressed, I'm all dressed, there's nothing else
for me to do.

[*Forlornly, almost fearfully.*]

I'm dressed, all dressed, nothing else for me to do. . . .

[*She moves about restlessly, aimlessly, and speaks, as if to
herself.*]

What am I—? Oh!—my bracelets. . . .

[*She starts working a collection of bracelets over her hands
onto her wrists, about six on each, as she talks.*]

I've thought a whole lot about it and now I know when I
made my mistake. Yes, I made my mistake when I told you
the truth about that thing with Skipper. Never should have
confessed it, a fatal error, tellin' you about that thing with
Skipper.

BRICK:
Maggie, shut up about Skipper. I mean it, Maggie; you got to
shut up about Skipper.

MARGARET:
You ought to understand that Skipper and I—

BRICK:
You don't think I'm serious, Maggie? You're fooled by the
fact that I am saying this quiet? Look, Maggie. What you're
doing is a dangerous thing to do. You're—you're—you're—
foolin' with something that—nobody ought to fool with.

MARGARET:
This time I'm going to finish what I have to say to you.
Skipper and I made love, if love you could call it, because it
made both of us feel a little bit closer to you. You see, you
son of a bitch, you asked too much of people, of me, of him,

56

of all the unlucky poor damned sons of bitches that happen to love you, and there was a whole pack of them, yes, there was a pack of them besides me and Skipper, you asked too goddam much of people that loved you, you—superior creature!—you godlike being!—And so we made love to each other to dream it was you, both of us! Yes, yes, yes! Truth, truth! What's so awful about it? I like it, I think the truth is—yeah! I shouldn't have told you. . . .

BRICK [*holding his head unnaturally still and uptilted a bit*]:
It was Skipper that told me about it. Not you, Maggie.

MARGARET:
I told you!

BRICK:
After he told me!

MARGARET:
What does it matter who—?

DIXIE:
I got your mallet, I got your mallet.

TRIXIE:
Give it to me, give it to me. IT's mine.

[*Brick turns suddenly out upon the gallery and calls:*]

BRICK:
Little girl! Hey, little girl!

LITTLE GIRL [*at a distance*]:
What, Uncle Brick?

BRICK:
Tell the folks to come up!—Bring everybody upstairs!

57

TRIXIE:
It's mine, it's mine.

MARGARET:
I can't stop myself! I'd go on telling you this in front of them all, if I had to!

BRICK:
Little girl! Go on, go on, will you? Do what I told you, call them!

DIXIE:
Okay.

MARGARET:
Because it's got to be told and you, you!—you never let me!

[*She sobs, then controls herself, and continues almost calmly.*]

It was one of those beautiful, ideal things they tell about in the Greek legends, it couldn't be anything else, you being you, and that's what made it so sad, that's what made it so awful, because it was love that never could be carried through to anything satisfying or even talked about plainly.

BRICK:
Maggie, you gotta stop this.

MARGARET:
Brick, I tell you, you got to believe me, Brick, I *do* understand all about it! I—I think it was—*noble!* Can't you tell I'm sincere when I say I respect it? My only point, the only point that I'm making, is life has got to be allowed to continue even after the *dream* of life is —all—over. . . .

[*Brick is without his crutch. Leaning on furniture, he crosses to pick it up as she continues as if possessed by a will outside herself:*]

Why I remember when we double-dated at college, Gladys
Fitzgerald and I and you and Skipper, it was more like a date
between you and Skipper. Gladys and I were just sort of
tagging along as 'if it was necessary to chaperone you!—to
make a good public impression—

BRICK [*turns to face her, half lifting his crutch*]:
Maggie, you want me to hit you with this crutch? Don't you
know I could kill you with this crutch?

MARGARET:
Good Lord, man, d' you think I'd care if you did?

BRICK:
One man has one great good true thing in his life. One great
good thing which is true!—I had friendship with Skipper.—
You are naming it dirty!

MARGARET:
I'm not naming it dirty! I am naming it clean.

BRICK:
Not love with you, Maggie, but friendship with Skipper was
that one great true thing, and you are naming it dirty!

MARGARET:
Then you haven't been listenin', not understood what I'm
saying! I'm naming it so damn clean that it killed poor
Skipper!—You two had something that had to be kept on
ice, yes, incorruptible, yes!—and death was the only icebox
where you could keep it....

BRICK:
I married you, Maggie. Why would I marry you, Maggie, if
I was—?

MARGARET:
Brick, let me finish!—I know, believe me I know, that it was

59

only Skipper that harbored even any *unconscious* desire for anything not perfectly pure between you two!—Now let me skip a little. You married me early that summer we graduated out of Ole Miss, and we were happy, weren't we, we were blissful, yes, hit heaven together ev'ry time that we loved! But that fall you an' Skipper turned down wonderful offers of jobs in order to keep on bein' football heroes—pro-football heroes. You organized the Dixie Stars that fall, so you could keep on bein' teammates forever! But somethin' was not right with it! —*Me included!*—between you. Skipper began hittin' the bottle . . . you got a spinal injury—couldn't play the Thanksgivin' game in Chicago, watched it on TV from a traction bed in Toledo. I joined Skipper. The Dixie Stars lost because poor Skipper was drunk. We drank together that night all night in the bar of the Blackstone and when cold day was comin' up over the Lake an' we were comin' out drunk to take a dizzy look at it, I said, "SKIPPER! STOP LOVIN' MY HUSBAND OR TELL HIM HE'S GOT TO LET YOU ADMIT IT TO HIM!"—one way or another!

HE SLAPPED ME HARD ON THE MOUTH!—then turned and ran without stopping once, I am sure, all the way back into his room at the Blackstone. . . .

—When I came to his room that night, with a little scratch like a shy little mouse at his door, he made that pitiful, ineffectual little attempt to prove that what I had said wasn't true. . . .

[*Brick strikes at her with crutch, a blow that shatters the gemlike lamp on the table.*]

—In this way, I destroyed him, by telling him truth that he and his world which he was born and raised in, yours and his world, had told him could not be told?

—From then on Skipper was nothing at all but a receptacle for liquor and drugs. . . .

—*Who shot cock robin? I with my—*

[She throws back her head with tight shut eyes.]

—*merciful arrow!*

[Brick strikes at her; misses.]

Missed me!—Sorry,—I'm not tryin' to whitewash my behavior, Christ, no! Brick, I'm not good. I don't know why people have to pretend to be good, nobody's good. The rich or the well-to-do can afford to respect moral patterns, conventional moral patterns, but I could never afford to, yeah, but— I'm honest! Give me credit for just that, will you *please?*— Born poor, raised poor, expect to die poor unless I manage to get us something out of what Big Daddy leaves when he dies of cancer! But Brick?!—*Skipper is dead! I'm alive!* Maggie the cat is—

[Brick hops awkwardly forward and strikes at her again with his crutch.]

—*alive! I am alive, alive! I am* . . .

[He hurls the crutch at her, across the bed she took refuge behind, and pitches forward on the floor as she completes her speech.]

—*alive!*

[A little girl, Dixie, bursts into the room, wearing an Indian war bonnet and firing a cap pistol at Margaret and shouting: "Bang, bang, bang!"]

[Laughter downstairs floats through the open hall door. Margaret had crouched gasping to bed at child's entrance. She now rises and says with cool fury:]

61

Little girl, your mother or someone should teach you—
[*gasping*]—to knock at a door before you come into a room.
Otherwise people might think that you—lack—good breeding. . . .

DIXIE:

Yanh, yanh, yanh, what is Uncle Brick doin' on th' floor?

BRICK:

I tried to kill your Aunt Maggie, but I failed—and I fell.
Little girl, give me my crutch so I can get up off th' floor.

MARGARET:

Yes, give your uncle his crutch, he's a cripple, honey, he broke
his ankle last night jumping hurdles on the high school
athletic field!

DIXIE:

What were you jumping hurdles for, Uncle Brick?

BRICK:

Because I used to jump them, and people like to do what they
used to do, even after they've stopped being able to do it. . . .

MARGARET:

That's right, that's your answer, now go away, little girl.

[*Dixie fires cap pistol at Margaret three times.*]

Stop, you stop that, monster! You little no-neck monster!

[*She seizes the cap pistol and hurls it through gallery
doors.*]

DIXIE [*with a precocious instinct for the cruelest thing*]:
You're *jealous!*—You're just jealous because you can't have
babies!

[*She sticks out her tongue at Margaret as she sashays past
her with her stomach stuck out, to the gallery. Margaret
slams the gallery doors and leans panting against them.*

62

There is a pause. Brick has replaced his spilt drink and sits, faraway, on the great four-poster bed.]

MARGARET:
You see?—they gloat over us being childless, even in front of their five little no-neck monsters!

[Pause. Voices approach on the stairs.]

Brick?—I've been to a doctor in Memphis, a—a gynecologist. . . .

I've been completely examined, and there is no reason why we can't have a child whenever we want one. And this is my time by the calendar to conceive. Are you listening to me? Are you? Are you LISTENING TO ME!

BRICK:
Yes. I hear you, Maggie.

[His attention returns to her inflamed face.]

—But how in hell on earth do you imagine—that you're going to have a child by a man that can't stand you?

MARGARET:
That's a problem that I will have to work out.

[She wheels about to face the hall door.]

MAE *[off stage left]*:
Come on, Big Daddy. We're all goin' up to Brick's room.

[From off stage left, voices: Reverend Tooker, Doctor Baugh, Mae.]

MARGARET:
Here they come!

[The lights dim.]

CURTAIN

ACT TWO

There is no lapse of time. Margaret and Brick are in the same positions they held at the end of Act I.

MARGARET [*at door*]:
Here they come!

[*Big Daddy appears first, a tall man with a fierce, anxious look, moving carefully not to betray his weakness even, or especially, to himself.*]

GOOPER:
I read in the *Register* that you're getting a new memorial window.

[*Some of the people are approaching through the hall, others along the gallery: voices from both directions. Gooper and Reverend Tooker become visible outside gallery doors, and their voices come in clearly.*]

[*They pause outside as Gooper lights a cigar.*]

REVEREND TOOKER [*vivaciously*]:
Oh, but St. Paul's in Grenada has three memorial windows, and the latest one is a Tiffany stained-glass window that cost twenty-five hundred dollars, a picture of Christ the Good Shepherd with a Lamb in His arms.

MARGARET:
Big Daddy.

BIG DADDY:
Well, Brick.

BRICK:
Hello Big Daddy.——Congratulations!

BIG DADDY:
——Crap. . . .

GOOPER:
Who give that window, Preach?

REVEREND TOOKER:
Clyde Fletcher's widow. Also presented St. Paul's with a baptismal font.

GOOPER:
Y'know what somebody ought t' give your church is a *coolin'* system, Preach.

MAE [*almost religiously*]:
—Let's see now, they've had their *tyyy*-phoid shots, and their tetanus shots, their diphtheria shots and their hepatitis shots and their polio shots, they got *those* shots every month from May through September, and—Gooper? Hey! Gooper!— What all have the kiddies been shot faw?

REVEREND TOOKER:
Yes, siree, Bob! And y'know what Gus Hamma's family gave in his memory to the church at Two Rivers? A complete new stone parish-house with a basketball court in the basement and a—

BIG DADDY [*uttering a loud barking laugh which is far from truly mirthful*]:
Hey, Preach! What's all this talk about memorials, Preach? Y' think somebody's about t' kick off around here? 'S that it?

[*Startled by this interjection, Reverend Tooker decides to laugh at the question almost as loud as he can.*

[*How he would answer the question we'll never know, as he's spared that embarrassment by the voice of Gooper's wife, Mae, rising high and clear as she appears with "Doc" Baugh, the family doctor, through the hall door.*]

66

MARGARET [*overlapping a bit*]:
Turn on the hi-fi, Brick! Let's have some music t' start off
th' party with!

BRICK:
You turn it on, Maggie.

[*The talk becomes so general that the room sounds like a
great aviary of chattering birds. Only Brick remains unen-
gaged, leaning upon the liquor cabinet with his faraway
smile, an ice cube in a paper napkin with which he now and
then rubs his forehead. He doesn't respond to Margaret's
command. She bounds forward and stoops over the instru-
ment panel of the console.*]

GOOPER:
We gave 'em that thing for a third anniversary present, got
three speakers in it.

[*The room is suddenly blasted by the climax of a Wag-
nerian opera or a Beethoven symphony.*]

BIG DADDY:
Turn that dam thing off!

[*Almost instant silence, almost instantly broken by the
shouting charge of Big Mama, entering through hall door
like a charging rhino.*]

BIG MAMA:
Wha's my Brick, wha's mah precious baby!!

BIG DADDY:
Sorry! Turn it back on!

[*Everyone laughs very loud. Big Daddy is famous for his
jokes at Big Mama's expense, and nobody laughs louder at
these jokes than Big Mama herself, though sometimes*

67

they're pretty cruel and Big Mama has to pick up or fuss with something to cover the hurt that the loud laugh doesn't quite cover.

[*On this occasion, a happy occasion because the dread in her heart has also been lifted by the false report on Big Daddy's condition, she giggles, grotesquely, coyly, in Big Daddy's direction and bears down upon Brick, all very quick and alive.*]

BIG MAMA:
Here he is, here's my precious baby! What's that you've got in your hand? You put that liquor down, son, your hand was made fo' holdin' somethin' better than that!

GOOPER:
Look at Brick put it down!

[*Brick has obeyed Big Mama by draining the glass and handing it to her. Again everyone laughs, some high, some low.*]

BIG MAMA:
Oh, you bad boy, you, you're my bad little boy. Give Big Mama a kiss, you bad boy, you!—Look at him shy away, will you? Brick never liked bein' kissed or made a fuss over, I guess because he's always had too much of it!

Son, you turn that thing off!

[*Brick has switched on the TV set.*]

I can't stand TV, radio was bad enough but TV has gone it one better, I mean—[*plops wheezing in chair*]—one worse, ha ha! Now what'm I sittin' down here faw? I want t' sit next to my sweetheart on the sofa, hold hands with him and love him up a little!

[*Big Mama has on a black and white figured chiffon. The
large irregular patterns, like the markings of some massive
animal, the luster of her great diamonds and many pearls,
the brilliants set in the silver frames of her glasses, her
riotous voice, booming laugh, have dominated the room
since she entered. Big Daddy has been regarding her with
a steady grimace of chronic annoyance.*]

BIG MAMA [*still louder*]:
Preacher, Preacher, hey, Preach! Give me you' hand an' help
me up from this chair!

REVEREND TOOKER:
None of your tricks, Big Mama!

BIG MAMA:
What tricks? You give me you' hand so I can get up an'—

[*Reverend Tooker extends her his hand. She grabs it and
pulls him into her lap with a shrill laugh that spans an
octave in two notes.*]

Ever seen a preacher in a fat lady's lap? Hey, hey, folks!
Ever seen a preacher in a fat lady's lap?

[*Big Mama is notorious throughout the Delta for this sort
of inelegant horseplay. Margaret looks on with indulgent
humor, sipping Dubonnet "on the rocks" and watching
Brick, but Mae and Gooper exchange signs of humorless
anxiety over these antics, the sort of behavior which Mae
thinks may account for their failure to quite get in with
the smartest young married set in Memphis, despite all.
One of the Negroes, Lacy or Sookey, peeks in, cackling.
They are waiting for a sign to bring in the cake and champagne. But Big Daddy's not amused. He doesn't understand
why, in spite of the infinite mental relief he's received from
the doctor's report, he still has these same old fox teeth*]

69

in his guts. "This spastic condition is something else," he says to himself, but aloud he roars at Big Mama:]

BIG DADDY:

BIG MAMA, WILL YOU QUIT HORSIN'?—You're too old an' too fat fo' that sort of crazy kid stuff an' besides a woman with your blood pressure—she had two hundred last spring! —is riskin' a stroke when you mess around like that. . . .

[*Mae blows on a pitch pipe.*]

BIG MAMA:

Here comes Big Daddy's birthday!

[*Negroes in white jackets enter with an enormous birthday cake ablaze with candles and carrying buckets of champagne with satin ribbons about the bottle necks.*

[*Mae and Gooper strike up song, and everybody, including the Negroes and Children, joins in. Only Brick remains aloof.*]

EVERYONE:

Happy birthday to you.
Happy birthday to you.
Happy birthday, Big Daddy—

[*Some sing: "Dear, Big Daddy!"*]

Happy birthday to you.

[*Some sing: "How old are you?"*]

[*Mae has come down center and is organizing her children like a chorus. She gives them a barely audible: "One, two, three!" and they are off in the new tune.*]

CHILDREN:

Skinamarinka—dinka—dink
Skinamarinka—do

We love you.
Skinamarinka—dinka—dink
Skinamarinka—do.

[*All together, they turn to Big Daddy.*]

Big Daddy, you!

[*They turn back front, like a musical comedy chorus.*]

We love you in the morning;
We love you in the night.
We love you when we're with you,
And we love you out of sight.
Skinamarinka—dinka—dink
Skinamarinka—do.

[*Mae turns to Big Mama.*]

Big Mama, too!

[*Big Mama bursts into tears. The Negroes leave.*]

BIG DADDY:
Now Ida, what the hell is the matter with you?

MAE:
She's just so happy.

BIG MAMA:
I'm just so happy, Big Daddy, I have to cry or something.

[*Sudden and loud in the hush:*]

Brick, do you know the wonderful news that Doc Baugh got from the clinic about Big Daddy? Big Daddy's one hundred per cent!

MARGARET:
Isn't that wonderful?

71

BIG MAMA:
He's just one hundred per cent. Passed the examination with flying colors. Now that we know there's nothing wrong with Big Daddy but a spastic colon, I can tell you something. I was worried sick, half out of my mind, for fear that Big Daddy might have a thing like—

[*Margaret cuts through this speech, jumping up and exclaiming shrilly:*]

MARGARET:
Brick, honey, aren't you going to give Big Daddy his birthday present?

[*Passing by him, she snatches his liquor glass from him.*

[*She picks up a fancily wrapped package.*]

Here it is, Big Daddy, this is from Brick!

BIG MAMA:
This is the biggest birthday Big Daddy's ever had, a hundred presents and bushels of telegrams from—

MAE [*at same time*]:
What is it, Brick?

GOOPER:
I bet 500 to 50 that Brick don't *know* what it is.

BIG MAMA:
The fun of presents is not knowing what they are till you open the package. Open your present, Big Daddy.

BIG DADDY:
Open it you'self. I want to ask Brick somethin! Come here, Brick.

MARGARET:
Big Daddy's callin' you, Brick.

[*She is opening the package.*]

BRICK:
Tell Big Daddy I'm crippled.

BIG DADDY:
I see you're crippled. I want to know how you got crippled.

MARGARET [*making diversionary tactics*]:
Oh, look, oh, look, why, it's a cashmere robe!

[*She holds the robe up for all to see.*]

MAE:
You sound surprised, Maggie.

MARGARET:
I never saw one before.

MAE:
That's funny.—*Hah!*

MARGARET [*turning on her fiercely, with a brilliant smile*]:
Why is it funny? All my family ever had was family—and luxuries such as cashmere robes still surprise me!

BIG DADDY [*ominously*]:
Quiet!

MAE [*heedless in her fury*]:
I don't see how you could be so surprised when you bought it yourself at Loewenstein's in Memphis last Saturday. You know how I know?

BIG DADDY:
I said, Quiet!

MAE:
—I know because the salesgirl that sold it to you waited on me and said, Oh, Mrs. Pollitt, your sister-in-law just bought a cashmere robe for your husband's father!

73

MARGARET:

Sister Woman! Your talents are wasted as a housewife and mother, you really ought to be with the FBI or—

BIG DADDY:

QUIET!

[*Reverend Tooker's reflexes are slower than the others'. He finishes a sentence after the bellow.*]

REVEREND TOOKER [*to Doc Baugh*]:

—the Stork and the Reaper are running neck and neck!

[*He starts to laugh gaily when he notices the silence and Big Daddy's glare. His laugh dies falsely.*]

BIG DADDY:

Preacher, I hope I'm not butting in on more talk about memorial stained-glass windows, am I, Preacher?

[*Reverend Tooker laughs feebly, then coughs dryly in the embarrassed silence.*]

Preacher?

BIG MAMA:

Now, Big Daddy, don't you pick on Preacher!

BIG DADDY [*raising his voice*]:

You ever hear that expression all hawk and no spit? You bring that expression to mind with that little dry cough of yours, all hawk an' no spit. . . .

[*The pause is broken only by a short startled laugh from Margaret, the only one there who is conscious of and amused by the grotesque.*]

MAE [*raising her arms and jangling her bracelets*]:

I wonder if the mosquitoes are active tonight?

BIG DADDY:
What's that, Little Mama? Did you make some remark?

MAE:
Yes, I said I wondered if the mosquitoes would eat us alive if we went out on the gallery for a while.

BIG DADDY:
Well, if they do, I'll have your bones pulverized for fertilizer!

BIG MAMA [*quickly*]:
Last week we had an airplane spraying the place and I think it done some good, at least I haven't had a—

BIG DADDY [*cutting her speech*]:
Brick, they tell me, if what they tell me is true, that you done some jumping last night on the high school athletic field?

BIG MAMA:
Brick, Big Daddy is talking to you, son.

BRICK [*smiling vaguely over his drink*]:
What was that, Big Daddy?

BIG DADDY:
They said you done some jumping on the high school track field last night.

BRICK:
That's what they told me, too.

BIG DADDY:
Was it jumping or humping that you were doing out there? What were doing out there at three A.M., layin' a woman on that cinder track?

BIG MAMA:
Big Daddy, you are off the sick-list, now, and I'm not going to excuse you for talkin' so—

BIG DADDY:
Quiet!

BIG MAMA:
—*nasty* in front of Preacher and—

BIG DADDY:
QUIET!—I ast you, Brick, if you was cuttin' you'self a piece o' poon-tang last night on that cinder track? I thought maybe you were chasin' poon-tang on that track an' tripped over something in the heat of the chase—'sthat it?

[*Gooper laughs, loud and false, others nervously following suit. Big Mama stamps her foot, and purses her lips, crossing to Mae and whispering something to her as Brick meets his father's hard, intent, grinning stare with a slow, vague smile that he offers all situations from behind the screen of his liquor.*]

BRICK:
No, sir, I don't think so. . . .

MAE [*at the same time, sweetly*]:
Reverend Tooker, let's you and I take a stroll on the widow's walk.

[*She and the preacher go out on the gallery as Big Daddy says:*]

BIG DADDY:
Then what the hell were you doing out there at three o'clock in the morning?

BRICK:
Jumping the hurdles, Big Daddy, runnin' and jumpin' the hurdles, but those high hurdles have gotten too high for me, now.

BIG DADDY:
Cause you was drunk?

BRICK [*his vague smile fading a little*]:
Sober I wouldn't have tried to jump the *low* ones. . . .

BIG MAMA [*quickly*]:
Big Daddy, blow out the candles on your birthday cake!

MARGARET [*at the same time*]:
I want to propose a toast to Big Daddy Pollitt on his sixty-fifth birthday, the biggest cotton planter in—

BIG DADDY [*bellowing with fury and disgust*]:
I told you to stop it, now stop it, quit this—!

BIG MAMA [*coming in front of Big Daddy with the cake*]:
Big Daddy, I will not allow you to talk that way, not even on your birthday, I—

BIG DADDY:
I'll talk like I want to on my birthday, Ida, or any other goddam day of the year and anybody here that don't like it knows what they can do!

BIG MAMA:
You don't mean that!

BIG DADDY:
What makes you think I don't mean it?

[*Meanwhile various discreet signals have been exchanged and Gooper has also gone out on the gallery.*]

BIG MAMA:
I just know you don't mean it.

BIG DADDY:
You don't know a goddam thing and you never did!

77

BIG MAMA:

Big Daddy, you don't mean that.

BIG DADDY:

Oh, yes, I do, oh, yes, I do, I mean it! I put up with a whole lot of crap around here because I thought I was dying. And you thought I was dying and you started taking over, well, you can stop taking over now, Ida, because I'm not gonna die, you can just stop now this business of taking over because you're not taking over because I'm not dying, I went through the laboratory and the goddam exploratory operation and there's nothing wrong with me but a spastic colon. And I'm not dying of cancer which you thought I was dying of. Ain't that so? Didn't you think that I was dying of cancer, Ida?

[*Almost everybody is out on the gallery but the two old people glaring at each other across the blazing cake.*

[*Big Mama's chest heaves and she presses a fat fist to her mouth.*

[*Big Daddy continues, hoarsely:*]

Ain't that so, Ida? Didn't you have an idea I was dying of cancer and now you could take control of this place and everything on it? I got that impression, I seemed to get that impression. Your loud voice everywhere, your fat old body butting in here and there!

BIG MAMA:

Hush! The Preacher!

BIG DADDY:

Fuck the goddam preacher!

[*Big Mama gasps loudly and sits down on the sofa which is almost too small for her.*]

78

Did you hear what I said? I said fuck the goddam preacher!

[*Somebody closes the gallery doors from outside just as there is a burst of fireworks and excited cries from the children.*]

BIG MAMA:
I never seen you act like this before and I can't think what's got in you!

BIG DADDY:
I went through all that laboratory and operation and all just so I would know if you or me was boss here! Well, now it turns out that I am and you ain't—and that's my birthday present—and my cake and champagne!—because for three years now you been gradually taking over. Bossing. Talking. Sashaying your fat old body around the place I made! I made this place! I was overseer on it! I was the overseer on the old Straw and Ochello plantation. I quit school at ten! I quit school at ten years old and went to work like a nigger in the fields. And I rose to be overseer of the Straw and Ochello plantation. And old Straw died and I was Ochello's partner and the place got bigger and bigger and bigger and bigger and bigger! I did all that myself with no goddam help from you, and now you think you're just about to take over. Well, I am just about to tell you that you are not just about to take over, you are not just about to take over a God damn thing. Is that clear to you, Ida? Is that very plain to you, now? Is that understood completely? I been through the laboratory from A to Z. I've had the goddam exploratory operation, and nothing is wrong with me but a spastic colon—made spastic, I guess, by *disgust!* By all the goddam lies and liars that I have had to put up with, and all the goddam hypocrisy that I lived with all these forty years that we been livin' together!

Hey! Ida!! Blow out the candles on the birthday cake! Purse

up your lips and draw a deep breath and blow out the goddam candles on the cake!

BIG MAMA:
Oh, Big Daddy, oh, oh, oh, Big Daddy!

BIG DADDY:
What's the matter with you?

BIG MAMA:
In all these years you never believed that I loved you??

BIG DADDY:
Huh?

BIG MAMA:
And I did, I did so much, I did love you!—I even loved your hate and your hardness, Big Daddy!

[*She sobs and rushes awkwardly out onto the gallery.*]

BIG DADDY [*to himself*]:
Wouldn't it be funny if that was true....

[*A pause is followed by a burst of light in the sky from the fireworks.*]

BRICK! HEY, BRICK!

[*He stands over his blazing birthday cake.*

[*After some moments, Brick hobbles in on his crutch, holding his glass.*

[*Margaret follows him with a bright, anxious smile.*]

I didn't call you, Maggie. I called Brick.

MARGARET:
I'm just delivering him to you.

[*She kisses Brick on the mouth which he immediately wipes with the back of his hand. She flies girlishly back out. Brick and his father are alone.*]

BIG DADDY:
Why did you do that?

BRICK:
Do what, Big Daddy?

BIG DADDY:
Wipe her kiss off your mouth like she'd spit on you.

BRICK:
I don't know. I wasn't conscious of it.

BIG DADDY:
That woman of yours has a better shape on her than Gooper's but somehow or other they got the same look about them.

BRICK:
What sort of look is that, Big Daddy?

BIG DADDY:
I don't know how to describe it but it's the same look.

BRICK:
They don't look peaceful, do they?

BIG DADDY:
No, they sure in hell don't.

BRICK:
They look nervous as cats?

BIG DADDY:
That's right, they look nervous as cats.

BRICK:
Nervous as a couple of cats on a hot tin roof?

BIG DADDY:

That's right, boy, they look like a couple of cats on a hot tin roof. It's funny that you and Gooper being so different would pick out the same type of woman.

BRICK:

Both of us married into society, Big Daddy.

BIG DADDY:

Crap . . . I wonder what gives them both that look?

BRICK:

Well. They're sittin' in the middle of a big piece of land, Big Daddy, twenty-eight thousand acres is a pretty big piece of land and so they're squaring off on it, each determined to knock off a bigger piece of it than the other whenever you let it go.

BIG DADDY:

I got a surprise for those women. I'm not gonna let it go for a long time yet if that's what they're waiting for.

BRICK:

That's right, Big Daddy. You just sit tight and let them scratch each other's eyes out. . . .

BIG DADDY:

You bet your life I'm going to sit tight on it and let those sons of bitches scratch their eyes out, ha ha ha. . . .

But Gooper's wife's a good breeder, you got to admit she's fertile. Hell, at supper tonight she had them all at the table and they had to put a couple of extra leafs in the table to make room for them, she's got five head of them, now, and another one's comin'.

BRICK:

Yep, number six is comin'. . . .

BIG DADDY:

Six hell, she'll probably drop a litter next time. Brick, you know, I swear to God, I don't know the way it happens?

BRICK:

The way what happens, Big Daddy?

BIG DADDY:

You git you a piece of land, by hook or crook, an' things start growin' on it, things accumulate on it, and the first thing you know it's completely out of hand, completely out of hand!

BRICK:

Well, they say nature hates a vacuum, Big Daddy.

BIG DADDY:

That's what they say, but sometimes I think that a vacuum is a hell of a lot better than some of the stuff that nature replaces it with.

Is someone out there by that door?

GOOPER:

Hey Mae.

BRICK:

Yep.

BIG DADDY:

Who?

[*He has lowered his voice.*]

BRICK:

Someone int'rested in what we say to each other.

BIG DADDY:

Gooper?——*GOOPER!*

[*After a discreet pause, Mae appears in the gallery door.*]

MAE:
Did you call Gooper, Big Daddy?

BIG DADDY:
Aw, it was you.

MAE:
Do you want Gooper, Big Daddy?

BIG DADDY:
No, and I don't want you. I want some privacy here, while I'm having a confidential talk with my son Brick. Now it's too hot in here to close them doors, but if I have to close those fuckin' doors in order to have a private talk with my son Brick, just let me know and I'll close 'em. Because I hate eavesdroppers, I don't like any kind of sneakin' an' spyin'.

MAE:
Why, Big Daddy—

BIG DADDY:
You stood on the wrong side of the moon, it threw your shadow!

MAE:
I was just—

BIG DADDY:
You was just nothing but *spyin'* an' you *know* it!

MAE [*begins to sniff and sob*]:
Oh, Big Daddy, you're so unkind for some reason to those that really love you!

BIG DADDY:
Shut up, shut up, shut up! I'm going to move you and Gooper out of that room next to this! It's none of your goddam business what goes on in here at night between Brick an' Maggie.

84

You listen at night like a couple of rutten peekhole spies and
go and give a report on what you hear to Big Mama an' she
comes to me and says they say such and such and so and so
about what they heard goin' on between Brick an' Maggie,
and Jesus, it makes me sick. I'm goin' to move you an' Gooper
out of that room, I can't stand sneakin' an' spyin', it makes
me puke. . . .

[*Mae throws back her head and rolls her eyes heavenward
and extends her arms as if invoking God's pity for this
unjust martyrdom; then she presses a handkerchief to her
nose and flies from the room with a loud swish of skirts.*]

BRICK [*now at the liquor cabinet*]:
They listen, do they?

BIG DADDY:
Yeah. They listen and give reports to Big Mama on what goes
on in here between you and Maggie. They say that—

[*He stops as if embarrassed.*]

—You won't sleep with her, that you sleep on the sofa. Is
that true or not true? If you don't like Maggie, get rid of
Maggie!—What are you doin' there now?

BRICK:
Fresh'nin' up my drink.

BIG DADDY:
Son, you know you got a real liquor problem?

BRICK:
Yes, sir, yes, I know.

BIG DADDY:
Is that why you quit sports-announcing, because of this liquor
problem?

BRICK:
Yes, sir, yes, sir, I guess so.

[*He smiles vaguely and amiably at his father across his replenished drink.*]

BIG DADDY:
Son, don't guess about it, it's too important.

BRICK [*vaguely*]:
Yes, sir.

BIG DADDY:
And listen to me, don't look at the damn chandelier. . . .

[*Pause. Big Daddy's voice is husky.*]

—Somethin' else we picked up at th' big fire sale in Europe.

[*Another pause.*]

Life is important. There's nothing else to hold onto. A man that drinks is throwing his life away. Don't do it, hold onto your life. There's nothing else to hold onto. . . .

Sit down over here so we don't have to raise our voices, the walls have ears in this place.

BRICK [*hobbling over to sit on the sofa beside him*]:
All right, Big Daddy.

BIG DADDY:
Quit!—how'd that come about? Some disappointment?

BRICK:
I don't know. Do you?

BIG DADDY:
I'm askin' you, God damn it! How in hell would I know if you don't?

BRICK:

I just got out there and found that I had a mouth full of cotton. I was always two or three beats behind what was goin' on on the field and so I—

BIG DADDY:

Quit!

BRICK [*amiably*]:

Yes, quit.

BIG DADDY:

Son?

BRICK:

Huh?

BIG DADDY [*inhales loudly and deeply from his cigar; then bends suddenly a little forward, exhaling loudly and raising a hand to his forehead*]:

—Whew!—ha ha!—I took in too much smoke, it made me a little lightheaded. . . .

[*The mantel clock chimes.*]

Why is it so damn hard for people to talk?

BRICK:

Yeah. . . .

[*The clock goes on sweetly chiming till it has completed the stroke of ten.*]

—Nice peaceful-soundin' clock, I like to hear it all night. . . .

[*He slides low and comfortable on the sofa; Big Daddy sits up straight and rigid with some unspoken anxiety. All his gestures are tense and jerky as he talks. He wheezes and pants and sniffs through his nervous speech, glancing quickly, shyly, from time to time, at his son.*]

BIG DADDY:
We got that clock the summer we wint to Europe, me an' Big Mama on that damn Cook's Tour, never had such an awful time in my life, I'm tellin' you, son, those gooks over there, they gouge your eyeballs out in their grand hotels. And Big Mama bought more stuff than you could haul in a couple of boxcars, that's no crap. Everywhere she wint on this whirlwind tour, she bought, bought, bought. Why, half that stuff she bought is still crated up in the cellar, under water last spring!

[He laughs.]

That Europe is nothin' on earth but a great big auction, that's all it is, that bunch of old worn-out places, it's just a big firesale, the whole fuckin' thing, an' Big Mama wint wild in it, why, you couldn't hold that woman with a mule's harness! Bought, bought, bought!—lucky I'm a rich man, yes siree, Bob, an' half that stuff is mildewin' in th' basement. It's lucky I'm a rich man, it sure is lucky, well, I'm a rich man, Brick, yep, I'm a mighty rich man.

[His eyes light up for a moment.]

Y'know how much I'm worth? Guess, Brick! Guess how much I'm worth!

[Brick smiles vaguely over his drink.]

Close on ten million in cash an' blue-chip stocks, outside, mind you, of twenty-eight thousand acres of the richest land this side of the valley Nile!

But a man can't buy his life with it, he can't buy back his life with it when his life has been spent, that's one thing not

88

offered in the Europe fire-sale or in the American markets or
any markets on earth, a man can't buy his life with it, he can't
buy back his life when his life is finished. . . .

That's a sobering thought, a very sobering thought, and that's
a thought that I was turning over in my head, over and over
and over—until today. . . .

I'm wiser and sadder, Brick, for this experience which I just
gone through. They's one thing else that I remember in
Europe.

BRICK:
What is that, Big Daddy?

BIG DADDY:
The hills around Barcelona in the country of Spain and the
children running over those bare hills in their bare skins
beggin' like starvin' dogs with howls and screeches, and how
fat the priests are on the streets of Barcelona, so many of them
and so fat and so pleasant, ha ha!—Y'know I could feed that
country? I got money enough to feed that goddam country,
but the human animal is a selfish beast and I don't reckon the
money I passed out there to those howling children in the
hills around Barcelona would more than upholster the chairs
in this room, I mean pay to put a new cover on this chair!

Hell, I threw them money like you'd scatter feed corn for
chickens, I threw money at them just to get rid of them long
enough to climb back into th' car and—drive away. . . .

And then in Morocco, them Arabs, why, I remember one
day in Marrakech, that old walled Arab city, I set on a broken-
down wall to have a cigar, it was fearful hot there and this
Arab woman stood in the road and looked at me till I was
embarrassed, she stood stock still in the dusty hot road and
looked at me till I was embarrassed. But listen to this. She had

a naked child with her, a little naked girl with her, barely able to toddle, and after a while she set this child on the ground and give her a push and whispered something to her.

This child come toward me, barely able t' walk, come toddling up to me and—

Jesus, it makes you sick t' remember a thing like this! It stuck out its hand and tried to unbutton my trousers!

That child was not yet five! Can you believe me? Or do you think that I am making this up? I wint back to the hotel and said to Big Mama, Git packed! We're clearing out of this country. . . .

BRICK:
Big Daddy, you're on a talkin' jag tonight.

BIG DADDY [*ignoring this remark*]:
Yes, sir, that's how it is, the human animal is a beast that dies but the fact that he's dying don't give him pity for others, no, sir, it—

—Did you say something?

BRICK:
Yes.

BIG DADDY:
What?

BRICK:
Hand me over that crutch so I can get up.

BIG DADDY:
Where you goin'?

BRICK:
I'm takin' a little short trip to Echo Spring.

BIG DADDY:
To where?

BRICK:
Liquor cabinet. . . .

BIG DADDY:
Yes, sir, boy—

[*He hands Brick the crutch.*]

—the human animal is a beast that dies and if he's got money
he buys and buys and buys and I think the reason he buys
everything he can buy is that in the back of his mind he has
the crazy hope that one of his purchases will be life everlasting!—Which it never can be. . . . The human animal is
a beast that—

BRICK [*at the liquor cabinet*]:
Big Daddy, you sure are shootin' th' breeze here tonight.

[*There is a pause and voices are heard outside.*]

BIG DADDY:
I been quiet here lately, spoke not a word, just sat and stared
into space. I had something heavy weighing on my mind but
tonight that load was took off me. That's why I'm talking.—
The sky looks diff'rent to me. . . .

BRICK:
You know what I like to hear most?

BIG DADDY:
What?

BRICK:
Solid quiet. Perfect unbroken quiet.

91

BIG DADDY:
Why?

BRICK:
Because it's more peaceful.

BIG DADDY:
Man, you'll hear a lot of that in the grave.

[*He chuckles agreeably.*]

BRICK:
Are you through talkin' to me?

BIG DADDY:
Why are you so anxious to shut me up?

BRICK:
Well, sir, ever so often you say to me, Brick, I want to have a talk with you, but when we talk, it never materializes. Nothing is said. You sit in a chair and gas about this and that and I look like I listen. I try to look like I listen, but I don't listen, not much. Communication is—awful hard between people an'—somehow between you and me, it just don't—happen.

BIG DADDY:
Have you ever been scared? I mean have you ever felt downright terror of something?

[*He gets up.*]

Just one moment.

[*He looks off as if he were going to tell an important secret.*]

BIG DADDY:
Brick?

BRICK:
What?

BIG DADDY:
Son, I thought I had it!

BRICK:
Had what? Had what, Big Daddy?

BIG DADDY:
Cancer!

BRICK:
Oh . . .

BIG DADDY:
I thought the old man made out of bones had laid his cold
and heavy hand on my shoulder!

BRICK:
Well, Big Daddy, you kept a tight mouth about it.

BIG DADDY:
A pig squeals. A man keeps a tight mouth about it, in spite
of a man not having a pig's advantage.

BRICK:
What advantage is that?

BIG DADDY:
Ignorance—of mortality—is a comfort. A man don't have
that comfort, he's the only living thing that conceives of
death, that knows what it is. The others go without knowing
which is the way that anything living should go, go without
knowing, without any knowledge of it, and yet a pig squeals,
but a man sometimes, he can keep a tight mouth about it.
Sometimes he—

93

[*There is a deep, smoldering ferocity in the old man.*]

—can keep a tight mouth about it. I wonder if—

BRICK:
What, Big Daddy?

BIG DADDY:
A whiskey highball would injure this spastic condition?

BRICK:
No, sir, it might do it good.

BIG DADDY [*grins suddenly, wolfishly*]:
*Jesus, I can't tell you! The sky is open! Christ, it's open
again! It's open, boy, it's open!*

[*Brick looks down at his drink.*]

BRICK:
You feel better, Big Daddy?

BIG DADDY:
Better? Hell! I can breathe!—All of my life I been like a
doubled up fist. . . .

[*He pours a drink.*]

—Poundin', smashin', drivin'!—now I'm going to loosen
these doubled-up hands and touch things *easy* with them. . . .

[*He spreads his hands as if caressing the air.*]

You know what I'm contemplating?

BRICK [*vaguely*]:
No, sir. What are you contemplating?

BIG DADDY:
Ha ha!—*Pleasure!*—pleasure with *women!*

94

[*Brick's smile fades a little but lingers.*]

—Yes, boy. I'll tell you something that you might not guess. I still have desire for women and this is my sixty-fifth birthday.

BRICK:
I think that's mighty remarkable, Big Daddy.

BIG DADDY:
Remarkable?

BRICK:
Admirable, Big Daddy.

BIG DADDY:
You're damn right it is, remarkable and admirable both. I realize now that I never had me enough. I let many chances slip by because of scruples about it, scruples, convention—crap. . . . All that stuff is bull, bull, bull!—It took the shadow of death to make me see it. Now that shadow's lifted, I'm going to cut loose and have, what is it they call it, have me a—ball!

BRICK:
A ball, huh?

BIG DADDY:
That's right, a ball, a ball! Hell!—I slept with Big Mama till, let's see, five years ago, till I was sixty and she was fifty-eight, and never even liked her, never did!

[*The phone has been ringing down the hall. Big Mama enters, exclaiming:*]

BIG MAMA:
Don't you men hear that phone ring? I heard it way out on the gall'ry.

BIG DADDY:

There's five rooms off this front gall'ry that you could go through. Why do you go through this one?

[*Big Mama makes a playful face as she bustles out the hall door.*]

Hunh!—Why, when Big Mama goes out of a room, I can't remember what that woman looks like—

BIG MAMA:

Hello.

BIG DADDY:

—But when Big Mama comes back into the room, boy, then I see what she looks like, and I wish I didn't!

[*Bends over laughing at this joke till it hurts his guts and he straightens with a grimace. The laugh subsides to a chuckle as he puts the liquor glass a little distrustfully down the table.*]

BIG MAMA:

Hello, Miss Sally.

[*Brick has risen and hobbled to the gallery doors.*]

BIG DADDY:

Hey! Where you goin'?

BRICK:

Out for a breather.

BIG DADDY:

Not yet you ain't. Stay here till this talk is finished, young fellow.

BRICK:

I thought it was finished, Big Daddy.

BIG DADDY:
It ain't even begun.

BRICK:
My mistake. Excuse me. I just wanted to feel that river breeze.

BIG DADDY:
Set back down in that chair.

[*Big Mama's voice rises, carrying down the hall.*]

BIG MAMA:
Miss Sally, you're a case! You're a caution, Miss Sally.

BIG DADDY:
Jesus, she's talking to my old maid sister again.

BIG MAMA:
Why didn't you give me a chance to explain it to you?

BIG DADDY:
Brick, this stuff burns me.

BIG MAMA:
Well, goodbye, now, Miss Sally. You come down real soon. Big Daddy's dying to see you.

BIG DADDY:
Crap!

BIG MAMA:
Yaiss, goodbye, Miss Sally. . . .

[*She hangs up and bellows with mirth. Big Daddy groans and covers his ears as she approaches.*

[*Bursting in:*]

Big Daddy, that was Miss Sally callin' from Memphis again! You know what she done, Big Daddy? She called her doctor in Memphis to git him to tell her what that spastic thing is! Ha-*HAAAA!*—And called back to tell me how relieved she was that—Hey! Let me in!

[*Big Daddy has been holding the door half closed against her.*]

BIG DADDY:

Naw I ain't. I told you not to come and go through this room. You just back out and go through those five other rooms.

BIG MAMA:

Big Daddy? Big Daddy? Oh, big Daddy!—You didn't mean those things you said to me, did you?

[*He shuts door firmly against her but she still calls.*]

Sweetheart? Sweetheart? Big Daddy? You didn't mean those awful things you said to me?—I know you didn't. I know you didn't mean those things in your heart. . . .

[*The childlike voice fades with a sob and her heavy footsteps retreat down the hall. Brick has risen once more on his crutches and starts for the gallery again.*]

BIG DADDY:

All I ask of that woman is that she leave me alone. But she can't admit to herself that she makes me sick. That comes of having slept with her too many years. Should of quit much sooner but that ,old woman she never got enough of it— and I was good in bed . . . I never should of wasted so much of it on her. . . . They say you got just so many and each one is numbered. Well, I got a few left in me, a few, and I'm going to pick me a good one to spend 'em on! I'm going to pick me a choice one, I don't care how much she costs, I'll smother her in—minks! Ha ha! I'll strip her naked and smother her in minks and choke her with diamonds! Ha ha!

I'll strip her naked and choke her with diamonds and smother her with minks and hump her from hell to breakfast. *Ha aha ha ha ha!*

MAE [*gaily at door*]:
Who's that laughin' in there?

GOOPER:
Is Big Daddy laughin' in there?

BIG DADDY:
Crap!—them two—*drips.* . . .

[*He goes over and touches Brick's shoulder.*]

Yes, son. Brick, boy.—I'm—*happy!* I'm happy, son, I'm happy!

[*He chokes a little and bites his under lip, pressing his head quickly, shyly against his son's head and then, coughing with embarrassment, goes uncertainly back to the table where he set down the glass. He drinks and makes a grimace as it burns his guts. Brick sighs and rises with effort.*]

What makes you so restless? Have you got ants in your britches?

BRICK:
Yes, sir . . .

BIG DADDY:
Why?

BRICK:
—Something—hasn't—happened. . . .

BIG DADDY:
Yeah? What is that!

BRICK [*sadly*]:
—the click. . . .

BIG DADDY:
Did you say click?

BRICK:
Yes, click.

BIG DADDY:
What click?

BRICK:
A click that I get in my head that makes me peaceful.

BIG DADDY:
I sure in hell don't know what you're talking about, but it disturbs me.

BRICK:
It's just a mechanical thing.

BIG DADDY:
What is a mechanical thing?

BRICK:
This click that I get in my head that makes me peaceful. I got to drink till I get it. It's just a mechanical thing, something like a—like a—like a—

BIG DADDY:
Like a—

BRICK:
Switch clicking off in my head, turning the hot light off and the cool night on and—

[*He looks up, smiling sadly.*]

—all of a sudden there's—peace!

BIG DADDY [*whistles long and soft with astonishment; he goes back to Brick and clasps his son's two shoulders*]:

Jesus! I didn't know it had gotten that bad with you. Why, boy, you're—*alcoholic!*

BRICK:
That's the truth, Big Daddy. I'm alcoholic.

BIG DADDY:
This shows how I—let things go!

BRICK:
I have to hear that little click in my head that makes me peaceful. Usually I hear it sooner than this, sometimes as early as—noon, but—

—Today it's—dilatory. . . .

—I just haven't got the right level of alcohol in my bloodstream yet!

[*This last statement is made with energy as he freshens his drink.*]

BIG DADDY:
Uh—huh. Expecting death made me blind. I didn't have no idea that a son of mine was turning into a drunkard under my nose.

BRICK [*gently*]:
Well, now you do, Big Daddy, the news has penetrated.

BIG DADDY:
UH-huh, yes, now I do, the news has—penetrated. . . .

BRICK:
And so if you'll excuse me—

BIG DADDY:
No, I won't excuse you.

BRICK:

—I'd better sit by myself till I hear that click in my head, it's just a mechanical thing but it don't happen except when I'm alone or talking to no one. . . .

BIG DADDY:

You got a long, long time to sit still, boy, and talk to no one, but now you're talkin' to me. At least I'm talking to you. And you set there and listen until I tell you the conversation is over!

BRICK:

But this talk is like all the others we've ever had together in our lives! It's nowhere, nowhere!—it's—it's *painful*, Big Daddy. . . .

BIG DADDY:

All right, then let it be painful, but don't you move from that chair!—I'm going to remove that crutch. . . .

[*He seizes the crutch and tosses it across room.*]

BRICK:

I can hop on one foot, and if I fall, I can crawl!

BIG DADDY:

If you ain't careful you're gonna crawl off this plantation and then, by Jesus, you'll have to hustle your drinks along Skid Row!

BRICK:

That'll come, Big Daddy.

BIG DADDY:

Naw, it won't. You're my son and I'm going to straighten you out; now that *I'm* straightened out, I'm going to straighten out you!

BRICK:
Yeah?

BIG DADDY:
Today the report come in from Ochsner Clinic. Y'know what they told me?

[His face glows with triumph.]

The only thing that they could detect with all the instruments of science in that great hospital is a little spastic condition of the colon! And nerves torn to pieces by all that worry about it.

[A little girl bursts into room with a sparkler clutched in each fist, hops and shrieks like a monkey gone mad and rushes back out again as Big Daddy strikes at her.

[Silence. The two men stare at each other. A woman laughs gaily outside.]

I want you to know I breathed a sigh of relief almost as powerful as the Vicksburg tornado!

[There is laughter outside, running footsteps, the soft, plushy sound and light of exploding rockets.

[Brick stares at him soberly for a long moment; then makes a sort of startled sound in his nostrils and springs up on one foot and hops across the room to grab his crutch, swinging on the furniture for support. He gets the crutch and flees as if in horror for the gallery. His father seizes him by the sleeve of his white silk pajamas.]

Stay here, you son of a bitch!—till I say go!

BRICK:
I can't.

103

BIG DADDY:

You sure in hell will, God damn it.

BRICK:

No, I can't. We talk, you talk, in—circles! We get no where, no where! It's always the same, you say you want to talk to me and don't have a fuckin' thing to say to me!

BIG DADDY:

Nothin' to say when I'm tellin' you I'm going to live when I thought I was dying?!

BRICK:

Oh—*that!*—Is that what you have to say to me?

BIG DADDY:

Why, you son of a bitch! Ain't that, ain't that—*important?!*

BRICK:

Well, you said that, that's said, and now I—

BIG DADDY:

Now you set back down.

BRICK:

You're all balled up, you—

BIG DADDY:

I ain't balled up!

BRICK:

You are, you're all balled up!

BIG DADDY:

Don't tell me what I am, you drunken whelp! I'm going to tear this coat sleeve off if you don't set down!

BRICK:

Big Daddy—

BIG DADDY:
Do what I tell you! I'm the boss here, now! I want you to
know I'm back in the driver's seat now!

[*Big Mama rushes in, clutching her great heaving bosom.*]

BIG MAMA:
Big Daddy!

BIG DADDY:
What in hell do you want in here, Big Mama?

BIG MAMA:
Oh, Big Daddy! Why are you shouting like that? I just cain't
stainnnnnnnd—it. . . .

BIG DADDY [*raising the back of his hand above his head*]:
GIT!—outa here.

[*She rushes back out, sobbing.*]

BRICK [*softly, sadly*]:
Christ. . . .

BIG DADDY [*fiercely*]:
Yeah! Christ!—is right . . .

[*Brick breaks loose and hobbles toward the gallery.*

[*Big Daddy jerks his crutch from under Brick so he steps
with the injured ankle. He utters a hissing cry of anguish,
clutches a chair and pulls it over on top of him on the
floor.*]

Son of a—tub of—hog fat. . . .

BRICK:
Big Daddy! Give me my crutch.

[*Big Daddy throws the crutch out of reach.*]

Give me that crutch, Big Daddy.

BIG DADDY:
Why do you drink?

BRICK:
Don't know, give me my crutch!

BIG DADDY:
You better think why you drink or give up drinking!

BRICK:
Will you please give me my crutch so I can get up off this floor?

BIG DADDY:
First you answer my question. Why do you drink? Why are you throwing your life away, boy, like somethin' disgusting you picked up on the street?

BRICK [*getting onto his knees*]:
Big Daddy, I'm in pain, I stepped on that foot.

BIG DADDY:
Good! I'm glad you're not too numb with the liquor in you to feel some pain!

BRICK:
You—spilled my—drink ...

BIG DADDY:
I'll make a bargain with you. You tell me why you drink and I'll hand you one. I'll pour you the liquor myself and hand it to you.

BRICK:
Why do I drink?

BIG DADDY:
Yea! Why?

BRICK:
Give me a drink and I'll tell you.

BIG DADDY:
Tell me first!

BRICK:
I'll tell you in one word.

BIG DADDY:
What word?

BRICK:
DISGUST!

[*The clock chimes softly, sweetly. Big Daddy gives it a short, outraged glance.*]

Now how about that drink?

BIG DADDY:
What are you disgusted with? You got to tell me that, first. Otherwise being disgusted don't make no sense!

BRICK:
Give me my crutch.

BIG DADDY:
You heard me, you got to tell me what I asked you first.

BRICK:
I told you, I said to kill my disgust!

BIG DADDY:
DISGUST WITH WHAT!

107

BRICK:
You strike a hard bargain.

BIG DADDY:
What are you disgusted with?—an' I'll pass you the liquor.

BRICK:
I can hop on one foot, and if I fall, I can crawl.

BIG DADDY:
You want liquor that bad?

BRICK [*dragging himself up, clinging to bedstead*]:
Yeah, I want it that bad.

BIG DADDY:
If I give you a drink, will you tell me what it is you're disgusted with, Brick?

BRICK:
Yes, sir, I will try to.

[*The old man pours him a drink and solemnly passes it to him.*

[*There is silence as Brick drinks.*]

Have you ever heard the word "mendacity"?

BIG DADDY:
Sure. Mendacity is one of them five dollar words that cheap politicians throw back and forth at each other.

BRICK:
You know what it means?

BIG DADDY:
Don't it mean lying and liars?

BRICK:
Yes, sir, lying and liars.

BIG DADDY:
Has someone been lying to you?

CHILDREN [*chanting in chorus offstage*]:
We want Big Dad-dee!
We want Big Dad-dee!

[*Gooper appears in the gallery door.*]

GOOPER:
Big Daddy, the kiddies are shouting for you out there.

BIG DADDY [*fiercely*]:
Keep out, Gooper!

GOOPER:
'Scuse *me!*

[*Big Daddy slams the doors after Gooper.*]

BIG DADDY:
Who's been lying to you, has Margaret been lying to you, has your wife been lying to you about something, Brick?

BRICK:
Not her. That wouldn't matter.

BIG DADDY:
Then who's been lying to you, and what about?

BRICK:
No one single person and no one lie. . . .

BIG DADDY:
Then what, what then, for Christ's sake?

BRICK:

—The whole, the whole—thing. . . .

BIG DADDY:

Why are you rubbing your head? You got a headache?

BRICK:

No, I'm tryin' to—

BIG DADDY:

—Concentrate, but you can't because your brain's all soaked with liquor, is that the trouble? Wet brain!

[*He snatches the glass from Brick's hand.*]

What do you know about this mendacity thing? Hell! I could write a book on it! Don't you know that? I could write a book on it and still not cover the subject? Well, I could, I could write a goddam book on it and still not cover the subject anywhere near enough!!—Think of all the lies I got to put up with!—Pretenses! Ain't that mendacity? Having to pretend stuff you don't think or feel or have any idea of? Having for instance to act like I care for Big Mama!—I haven't been able to stand the sight, sound, or smell of that woman for forty years now!—even when I *laid* her!—regular as a piston. . . .

Pretend to love that son of a bitch of a Gooper and his wife Mae and those five same screechers out there like parrots in a jungle? Jesus! Can't stand to look at 'em!

Church!—it bores the bejesus out of me but I go!—I go an' sit there and listen to the fool preacher!

Clubs!—Elks! Masons! Rotary!—*crap!*

[*A spasm of pain makes him clutch his belly. He sinks into a chair and his voice is softer and hoarser.*]

110

You I *do* like for some reason, did always have some kind of real feeling for—affection—respect—yes, always. . . .

You and being a success as a planter is all I ever had any devotion to in my whole life!—and that's the truth. . . .

I don't know why, but it is!

I've lived with mendacity!—Why can't *you* live with it? Hell, you *got* to live with it, there's nothing *else* to *live* with except mendacity, is there?

BRICK:
Yes, sir. Yes, sir there is something else that you can live with!

BIG DADDY:
What?

BRICK [*lifting his glass*]:
This!—Liquor. . . .

BIG DADDY:
That's not living, that's dodging away from life.

BRICK:
I want to dodge away from it.

BIG DADDY:
Then why don't you kill yourself, man?

BRICK:
I like to drink. . . .

BIG DADDY:
Oh, God, I can't talk to you. . . .

BRICK:
I'm sorry, Big Daddy.

BIG DADDY:

Not as sorry as I am. I'll tell you something. A little while back when I thought my number was up—

[*This speech should have torrential pace and fury.*]

—before I found out it was just this—spastic—colon. I thought about you. Should I or should I not, if the jig was up, give you this place when I go—since I hate Gooper an' Mae an' know that they hate me, and since all five same monkeys are little Maes an' Goopers.—And I thought, No!—Then I thought, Yes!—I couldn't make up my mind. I hate Gooper and his five same monkeys and that bitch Mae! Why should I turn over twenty-eight thousand acres of the richest land this side of the valley Nile to not my kind?—But why in hell, on the other hand, Brick—should I subsidize a goddam fool on the bottle?—Liked or not liked, well, maybe even—*loved!* —Why should I do that?—Subsidize worthless behavior? Rot? Corruption?

BRICK [*smiling*]:

I understand.

BIG DADDY:

Well, if you do, you're smarter than I am, God damn it, because I don't understand. And this I will tell you frankly. I didn't make up my mind at all on that question and still to this day I ain't made out no will!—Well, now I don't *have* to. The pressure is gone. I can just wait and see if you pull yourself together or if you don't.

BRICK:

That's right, Big Daddy.

BIG DADDY:

You sound like you thought I was kidding.

112

BRICK [*rising*]:
No, sir, I know you're not kidding.

BIG DADDY:
But you don't care—?

BRICK [*hobbling toward the gallery door*]:
No, sir, I don't care. . . .

[*He stands in the gallery doorway as the night sky turns pink and green and gold with successive flashes of light.*]

BIG DADDY:
WAIT!—Brick. . . .

[*His voice drops. Suddenly there is something shy, almost tender, in his restraining gesture.*]

Don't let's—leave it like this, like them other talks we've had, we've always—talked around things, we've—just talked around things for some fuckin' reason, I don't know what, it's always like something was left not spoken, something avoided because neither of us was honest enough with the—other. . . .

BRICK:
I never lied to you, Big Daddy.

BIG DADDY:
Did I ever to *you?*

BRICK:
No, sir. . . .

BIG DADDY:
Then there is at least two people that never lied to each other.

BRICK:
But we've never *talked* to each other.

BIG DADDY:
We can *now*.

BRICK:
Big Daddy, there don't seem to be anything much to say.

BIG DADDY:
You say that you drink to kill your disgust with lying.

BRICK:
You said to give you a reason.

BIG DADDY:
Is liquor the only thing that'll kill this disgust?

BRICK:
Now. Yes.

BIG DADDY:
But not once, huh?

BRICK:
Not when I was still young an' believing. A drinking man's someone who wants to forget he isn't still young an' believing.

BIG DADDY:
Believing what?

BRICK:
Believing. . . .

BIG DADDY:
Believing *what?*

BRICK [*stubbornly evasive*]:
Believing. . . .

BIG DADDY:
I don't know what the hell you mean by believing and I don't

114

think you know what you mean by believing, but if you still got sports in your blood, go back to sports announcing and—

BRICK:
Sit in a glass box watching games I can't play? Describing what I can't do while players do it? Sweating out their disgust and confusion in contests I'm not fit for? Drinkin' a coke, half bourbon, so I can stand it? That's no goddam good any more, no help—time just outran me, Big Daddy—got there first . . .

BIG DADDY:
I think you're passing the buck.

BRICK:
You know many drinkin' men?

BIG DADDY [*with a slight, charming smile*]:
I have known a fair number of that species.

BRICK:
Could any of them tell you why he drank?

BIG DADDY:
Yep, you're passin' the buck to things like time and disgust with "mendacity" and—crap!—if you got to use that kind of language about a thing, it's ninety-proof bull, and I'm not buying any.

BRICK:
I had to give you a reason to get a drink!

BIG DADDY:
You started drinkin' when your friend Skipper died.

[*Silence for five beats. Then Brick makes a startled move-ment, reaching for his crutch.*]

BRICK:

What are you suggesting?

BIG DADDY:

I'm suggesting nothing.

[*The shuffle and clop of Brick's rapid hobble away from his father's steady, grave attention.*]

—But Gooper an' Mae suggested that there was something not right exactly in your—

BRICK [*stopping short downstage as if backed to a wall*]: "Not right"?

BIG DADDY:

Not, well, exactly *normal* in your friendship with—

BRICK:

They suggested that, too? I thought that was Maggie's suggestion.

[*Brick's detachment is at last broken through. His heart is accelerated; his forehead sweat-beaded; his breath becomes more rapid and his voice hoarse. The thing they're discussing, timidly and painfully on the side of Big Daddy, fiercely, violently on Brick's side, is the inadmissible thing that Skipper died to disavow between them. The fact that if it existed it had to be disavowed to "keep face" in the world they lived in, may be at the heart of the "mendacity" that Brick drinks to kill his disgust with. It may be the root of his collapse. Or maybe it is only a single manifestation of it, not even the most important. The bird that I hope to catch in the net of this play is not the solution of one man's psychological problem. I'm trying to catch the true quality of experience in a group of people, that cloudy, flickering, evanescent—fiercely charged!—interplay of live*]

*human beings in the thundercloud of a common crisis.
Some mystery should be left in the revelation of character
in a play, just as a great deal of mystery is always left in
the revelation of character in life, even in one's own character to himself. This does not absolve the playwright of his
duty to observe and probe as clearly and deeply as he* legiti-
mately *can: but it should steer him away from "pat" con-
clusions, facile definitions which make a play just a play,
not a snare for the truth of human experience.*

*[The following scene should be played with great concen-
tration, with most of the power leashed but palpable in
what is left unspoken.]*

Who else's suggestion is it, is it *yours?* How many others
thought that Skipper and I were—

BIG DADDY [*gently*]:
Now, hold on, hold on a minute, son.—I knocked around in
my time.

BRICK:
What's that got to do with—

BIG DADDY:
I said "Hold on!"—I bummed, I bummed this country till I
was—

BRICK:
Whose suggestion, who else's suggestion is it?

BIG DADDY:
Slept in hobo jungles and railroad Y's and flophouses in all
cities before I—

BRICK:
Oh, *you* think so, too, you call me your son and a queer. Oh!

117

Maybe that's why you put Maggie and me in this room that was Jack Straw's and Peter Ochello's, in which that pair of old sisters slept in a double bed where both of 'em died!

BIG DADDY:
Now just don't go throwing rocks at—

[*Suddenly Reverend Tooker appears in the gallery doors, his head slightly, playfully, fatuously cocked, with a practised clergyman's smile, sincere as a bird call blown on a hunter's whistle, the living embodiment of the pious, conventional lie.*

[*Big Daddy gasps a little at this perfectly timed, but incongruous, apparition.*]

—What're you lookin' for, Preacher?

REVEREND TOOKER:
The gentleman's lavatory, ha ha!—heh, heh . . .

BIG DADDY [*with strained courtesy*]:
—Go back out and walk down to the other end of the gallery, Reverend Tooker, and use the bathroom connected with my bedroom, and if you can't find it, ask them where it is!

REVEREND TOOKER:
Ah, thanks.

[*He goes out with a deprecatory chuckle.*]

BIG DADDY:
It's hard to talk in this place . . .

BRICK:
Son of a—!

BIG DADDY [*leaving a lot unspoken*]:
—I seen all things and understood a lot of them, till 1910. Christ, the year that—I had worn my shoes through, hocked

118

my—I hopped off a yellow dog freight car half a mile down the road, slept in a wagon of cotton outside the gin—Jack Straw an' Peter Ochello took me in. Hired me to manage this place which grew into this one.—When Jack Straw died— why, old Peter Ochello quit eatin' like a dog does when its master's dead, and died, too!

BRICK:
Christ!

BIG DADDY:
I'm just saying I understand such—

BRICK [*violently*]:
Skipper is dead. I have not quit eating!

BIG DADDY:
No, but you started drinking.

[*Brick wheels on his crutch and hurls his glass across the room shouting.*]

BRICK:
YOU THINK SO, TOO?

[*Footsteps run on the gallery. There are women's calls.*

[*Big Daddy goes toward the door.*]

[*Brick is transformed, as if a quiet mountain blew suddenly up in volcanic flame.*]

BRICK:
You think so, too? You think so, too? You think me an' Skipper did, did, did!—*sodomy!*—together?

BIG DADDY:
Hold—!

BRICK:
That what you—

BIG DADDY:
—*ON*—a minute!

BRICK:
You think we did dirty things between us, Skipper an'—

BIG DADDY:
Why are you shouting like that? Why are you—

BRICK:
—Me, is that what you think of Skipper, is that—

BIG DADDY:
—so excited? I don't think nothing. I don't know nothing. I'm simply telling you what—

BRICK:
You think that Skipper and me were a pair of dirty old men?

BIG DADDY:
Now that's—

BRICK:
Straw? Ochello? A couple of—

BIG DADDY:
Now just—

BRICK:
—fucking sissies? Queers? Is that what you—

BIG DADDY:
Shhh.

BRICK:
—think?

[*He loses his balance and pitches to his knees without noticing the pain. He grabs the bed and drags himself up.*]

120

BIG DADDY:
Jesus!—Whew.... Grab my hand!

BRICK:
Naw, I don't want your hand....

BIG DADDY:
Well, I want yours. Git up!

[*He draws him up, keeps an arm about him with concern and affection.*]

You broken out in a sweat! You're panting like you'd run a race with—

BRICK [*freeing himself from his father's hold*]:
Big Daddy, you shock me, Big Daddy, you, you—*shock* me! Talkin' so—

[*He turns away from his father.*]

—casually!—about a—thing like that ...

—Don't you know how people *feel* about things like that? How, how *disgusted* they are by things like that? Why, at Ole Miss when it was discovered a pledge to our fraternity, Skipper's and mine, did a, *attempted* to do a, unnatural thing with—

We not only dropped him like a hot rock!—We told him to git off the campus, and he did, he got!—All the way to—

[*He halts, breathless.*]

BIG DADDY:
—Where?

BRICK:
—North Africa, last I heard!

BIG DADDY:

Well, I have come back from further away than that, I have just now returned from the other side of the moon, death's country, son, and I'm not easy to shock by anything here.

[*He comes downstage and faces out.*]

Always, anyhow, lived with too much space around me to be infected by ideas of other people. One thing you can grow on a big place more important than cotton!—is *tolerance!*—I grown it.

[*He returns toward Brick.*]

BRICK:

Why can't exceptional friendship, *real, real, deep, deep friendship!* between two men be respected as something clean and decent without being thought of as—

BIG DADDY:

It can, it is, for God's sake.

BRICK:

—*Fairies.* . . .

[*In his utterance of this word, we gauge the wide and profound reach of the conventional mores he got from the world that crowned him with early laurel.*]

BIG DADDY:

I told Mae an' Gooper—

BRICK:

Frig Mae and Gooper, frig all dirty lies and liars!—Skipper and me had a clean, true thing between us!—had a clean friendship, practically all our lives, till Maggie got the idea you're talking about. Normal? No!—It was too rare to be normal, any true thing between two people is too rare to be

normal. Oh, once in a while he put his hand on my shoulder
or I'd put mine on his, oh, maybe even, when we were touring
the country in pro-football an' shared hotel-rooms we'd reach
across the space between the two beds and shake hands to say
goodnight, yeah, one or two times we—

BIG DADDY:
Brick, nobody thinks that that's not normal!

BRICK:
Well, they're mistaken, it was! It was a pure an' true thing
an' that's not normal.

MAE [*off stage*]:
Big Daddy, they're startin' the fireworks.

[*They both stare straight at each other for a long moment.
The tension breaks and both turn away as if tired.*]

BIG DADDY:
Yeah, it's—hard t'—talk. . . .

BRICK:
All right, then, let's—let it go. . . .

BIG DADDY:
Why did Skipper crack up? Why have you?

[*Brick looks back at his father again. He has already decided, without knowing that he has made this decision,
that he is going to tell his father that he is dying of cancer.
Only this could even the score between them: one inadmissible thing in return for another.*]

BRICK [*ominously*]:
All right. You're asking for it, Big Daddy. We're finally going
to have that real true talk you wanted. It's too late to stop it,
now, we got to carry it through and cover every subject.

123

[*He hobbles back to the liquor cabinet.*]

Uh-huh.

[*He opens the ice bucket and picks up the silver tongs with slow admiration of their frosty brightness.*]

Maggie declares that Skipper and I went into pro-football after we left "Ole Miss" because we were scared to grow up . . .

[*He moves downstage with the shuffle and clop of a cripple on a crutch. As Margaret did when her speech became "recitative," he looks out into the house, commanding its attention by his direct, concentrated gaze—a broken, "tragically elegant" figure telling simply as much as he knows of "the Truth":*]

—Wanted to—keep on tossing—those long, long!—high, high!—passes that—couldn't be intercepted except by time, the aerial attack that made us famous! And so we did, we did, we kept it up for one season, that aerial attack, we held it high!—Yeah, but—

—that summer, Maggie, she laid the law down to me, said, Now or never, and so I married Maggie. . . .

BIG DADDY:
How was Maggie in bed?

BRICK [*wryly*]:
Great! the greatest!

[*Big Daddy nods as if he thought so.*]

She went on the road that fall with the Dixie Stars. Oh, she made a great show of being the world's best sport. She wore a—wore a—tall bearskin cap! A shako, they call it, a dyed moleskin coat, a moleskin coat dyed red!—Cut up crazy!

124

Rented hotel ballrooms for victory celebrations, wouldn't cancel them when it—turned out—defeat. . . .

MAGGIE THE CAT! Ha ha!

[*Big Daddy nods.*]

—But Skipper, he had some fever which came back on him which doctors couldn't explain and I got that injury—turned out to be just a shadow on the X-ray plate—and a touch of bursitis. . . .

I lay in a hospital bed, watched our games on TV, saw Maggie on the bench next to Skipper when he was hauled out of a game for stumbles, fumbles!—Burned me up the way she hung on his arm!—Y'know, I think that Maggie had always felt sort of left out because she and me never got any closer together than two people just get in bed, which is not much closer than two cats on a—fence humping. . . .

So! She took this time to work on poor dumb Skipper. He was a less than average student at Ole Miss, you know that, don't you?!—Poured in his mind the dirty, false idea that what we were, him and me, was a frustrated case of that ole pair of sisters that lived in this room, Jack Straw and Peter Ochello!—He, poor Skipper, went to bed with Maggie to prove it wasn't true, and when it didn't work out, he thought it *was* true!—Skipper broke in two like a rotten stick—nobody ever turned so fast to a lush—or died of it so quick. . . .

—Now are you satisfied?

[*Big Daddy has listened to this story, dividing the grain from the chaff. Now he looks at his son.*]

BIG DADDY:
Are *you* satisfied?

125

BRICK:
With what?

BIG DADDY:
That half-ass story!

BRICK:
What's half-ass about it?

BIG DADDY:
Something's left out of that story. What did you leave out?

[*The phone has started ringing in the hall.*]

GOOPER [*off stage*]:
Hello.

[*As if it reminded him of something, Brick glances suddenly toward the sound and says:*]

BRICK:
Yes!—I left out a long-distance call which I had from Skipper—

GOOPER:
Speaking, go ahead.

BRICK:
—In which he made a drunken confession to me and on which I hung up!

GOOPER:
No.

BRICK:
—Last time we spoke to each other in our lives . . .

GOOPER:
No, sir.

BIG DADDY:
You musta said something to him before you hung up.

BRICK:
What could I say to him?

BIG DADDY:
Anything. Something.

BRICK:
Nothing.

BIG DADDY:
Just hung up?

BRICK:
Just hung up.

BIG DADDY:
Uh-huh. Anyhow now!—we have tracked down the lie with which you're disgusted and which you are drinking to kill your disgust with, Brick. You been passing the buck. This disgust with mendacity is disgust with yourself.

You!—dug the grave of your friend and kicked him in it!—before you'd face truth with him!

BRICK:
His truth, not *mine!*

BIG DADDY:
His truth, okay! But you wouldn't face it with him!

BRICK:
Who *can* face truth? Can *you?*

BIG DADDY:
Now don't start passin' the rotten buck again, boy!

127

BRICK:

How about these birthday congratulations, these many, many happy returns of the day, when ev'rybody knows there won't be any except you!

[*Gooper, who has answered the hall phone, lets out a high, shrill laugh; the voice becomes audible saying: "No, no, you got it all wrong! Upside down! Are you crazy?"*]
[*Brick suddenly catches his breath as he realized that he has made a shocking disclosure. He hobbles a few paces, then freezes, and without looking at his father's shocked face, says:*]

Let's, let's—go out, now, and—watch the fireworks. Come on, Big Daddy.

[*Big Daddy moves suddenly forward and grabs hold of the boy's crutch like it was a weapon for which they were fighting for possession.*]

BIG DADDY:

Oh, no, no! No one's going out! What did you start to say?

BRICK:

I don't remember.

BIG DADDY:

"Many happy returns when they know there won't be any"?

BRICK:

Aw, hell, Big Daddy, forget it. Come on out on the gallery and look at the fireworks they're shooting off for your birthday. . . .

BIG DADDY:

First you finish that remark you were makin' before you cut off. "Many happy returns when they know there won't be any"?—Ain't that what you just said?

BRICK:

Look, now. I can get around without that crutch if I have to but it would be a lot easier on the furniture an' glassware if I didn' have to go swinging along like Tarzan of th'—

BIG DADDY:

FINISH! WHAT YOU WAS SAYIN'!

[*An eerie green glow shows in sky behind him.*]

BRICK [*sucking the ice in his glass, speech becoming thick*]:
Leave th' place to Gooper and Mae an' their five little same little monkeys. All I want is—

BIG DADDY:

"LEAVE TH' PLACE," did you say?

BRICK [*vaguely*]:
All twenty-eight thousand acres of the richest land this side of the valley Nile.

BIG DADDY:

Who said I was "leaving the place" to Gooper or anybody? This is my sixty-fifth birthday! I got fifteen years or twenty years left in me! I'll outlive *you!* I'll bury you an' have to pay for your coffin!

BRICK:

Sure. Many happy returns. Now let's go watch the fireworks, come on, let's—

BIG DADDY:

Lying, have they been lying? About the report from th'— clinic? Did they, did they—find something?—*Cancer*. Maybe?

BRICK:

Mendacity is a system that we live in. Liquor is one way out an' death's the other. . . .

[*He takes the crutch from Big Daddy's loose grip and swings out on the gallery leaving the doors open.*

[*A song, "Pick a Bale of Cotton," is heard.*]

MAE [*appearing in door*]:
Oh, Big Daddy, the field hands are singin' fo' you!

BRICK:
I'm sorry, Big Daddy. My head don't work any more and it's hard for me to understand how anybody could care if he lived or died or was dying or cared about anything but whether or not there was liquor left in the bottle and so I said what I said without thinking. In some ways I'm no better than the others, in some ways worse because I'm less alive. Maybe it's being alive that makes them lie, and being almost *not* alive makes me sort of accidentally truthful—I don't know but—anyway—we've been friends . . .

—And being friends is telling each other the truth. . . .

[*There is a pause.*]

You told *me!* I told *you!*

BIG DADDY [*slowly and passionately*]:
CHRIST—DAMN—

GOOPER [*off stage*]:
Let her go!

[*Fireworks off stage right.*]

BIG DADDY:
—ALL—LYING SONS OF—LYING BITCHES!

[*He straightens at last and crosses to the inside door. At the door he turns and looks back as if he had some des-*

*perate question he couldn't put into words. Then he nods
reflectively and says in a hoarse voice:*]

Yes, all liars, all liars, all lying dying liars!

[*This is said slowly, slowly, with a fierce revulsion. He goes
on out.*]

—Lying! Dying! Liars!

[*Brick remains motionless as the lights dim out and the
curtain falls.*]

CURTAIN

ACT THREE

BIG DADDY:
ALL LYIN'—DYIN'!—LIARS! LIARS!—LIARS!

[*Margaret enters.*]

MARGARET:
Brick, what in the name of God was goin' on in this room?

[*Dixie and Trixie enter through the doors and circle around Margaret shouting. Mae enters from the lower gallery window.*]

MAE:
Dixie, Trixie, you quit that!

[*Gooper enters through the doors.*]

Gooper, will y' please get these kiddies to bed right now!

GOOPER:
Mae, you seen Big Mama?

MAE:
Not yet.

[*Gooper and kids exit through the doors. Reverend Tooker enters through the windows.*]

REVEREND TOOKER:
Those kiddies are so full of vitality. I think I'll have to be starting back to town.

MAE:
Not yet, Preacher. You know we regard you as a member of this family, one of our closest an' dearest, so you just got t' be with

us when Doc Baugh gives Big Mama th' actual truth about th' report from the clinic.

MARGARET:
Where do you think you're going?

BRICK:
Out for some air.

MARGARET:
Why'd Big Daddy shout "Liars"?

MAE:
Has Big Daddy gone to bed, Brick?

GOOPER [*entering*]:
Now where is that old lady?

REVEREND TOOKER:
I'll look for her.

[*He exits to the gallery.*]

MAE:
Cain'tcha find her, Gooper?

GOOPER:
She's avoidin' this talk.

MAE:
I think she senses somethin'.

MARGARET [*going out on the gallery to Brick*]:
Brick, they're goin' to tell Big Mama the truth about Big Daddy and she's goin' to need you.

DOCTOR BAUGH:
This is going to be painful.

MAE:
Painful things caint always be avoided.

REVEREND TOOKER:
I see Big Mama.

GOOPER:
Hey, Big Mama, come here.

MAE:
Hush, Gooper, don't holler.

BIG MAMA [*entering*]:
Too much smell of burnt fireworks makes me feel a little bit sick at my stomach.—Where is Big Daddy?

MAE:
That's what I want to know, where has Big Daddy gone?

BIG MAMA:
He must have turned in, I reckon he went to baid . . .

GOOPER:
Well, then, now we can talk.

BIG MAMA:
What *is* this talk, *what* talk?

[*Margaret appears on the gallery, talking to Doctor Baugh.*]

MARGARET [*musically*]:
My family freed their slaves ten years before abolition. My great-great-grandfather gave his slaves their freedom five years before the War between the States started!

MAE:
Oh, for God's sake! Maggie's climbed back up in her family tree!

MARGARET [*sweetly*]:
What, Mae?

[*The pace must be very quick: great Southern animation.*]

135

BIG MAMA [*addressing them all*]:
I think Big Daddy was just worn out. He loves his family, he loves to have them around him, but it's a strain on his nerves. He wasn't himself tonight, Big Daddy wasn't himself, I could tell he was all worked up.

REVEREND TOOKER:
I think he's remarkable.

BIG MAMA:
Yaisss! Just remarkable. Did you all notice the food he ate at that table? Did you all notice the supper he put away? Why he ate like a hawss!

GOOPER:
I hope he doesn't regret it.

BIG MAMA:
What? Why that man—ate a huge piece of cawn bread with molasses on it! Helped himself twice to hoppin' John.

MARGARET:
Big Daddy loves hoppin' John.—We had a real country dinner.

BIG MAMA [*overlapping Margaret*]:
Yaiss, he simply adores it! an' candied yams? Son? That man put away enough food at that table to stuff a *field* hand!

GOOPER [*with grim relish*]:
I hope he don't have to pay for it later on . . .

BIG MAMA [*fiercely*]:
What's *that*, Gooper?

MAE:
Gooper says he hopes Big Daddy doesn't suffer tonight.

136

BIG MAMA:
Oh, shoot, Gooper says, Gooper says! Why should Big Daddy suffer for satisfying a normal appetite? There's nothin' wrong with that man but nerves, he's sound as a dollar! And now he knows he is an' that's why he ate such a supper. He had a big load off his mind, knowin' he wasn't doomed t'—what he thought he was doomed to . . .

MARGARET [*sadly and sweetly*]:
Bless his old sweet soul . . .

BIG MAMA [*vaguely*]:
Yais, bless his heart, where's Brick?

MAE:
Outside.

GOOPER:
—Drinkin' . . .

BIG MAMA:
I know he's drinkin'. Cain't I see he's drinkin' without you continually tellin' me that boy's drinkin'?

MARGARET:
Good for you, Big Mama!

[*She applauds.*]

BIG MAMA:
Other people *drink* and *have* drunk an' will *drink*, as long as they make that stuff an' put it in bottles.

MARGARET:
That's the truth. I never trusted a man that didn't drink.

BIG MAMA:
Brick? Brick!

137

MARGARET:
He's still on the gall'ry. I'll go bring him in so we can talk.

BIG MAMA [*Worriedly*]:
I don't know what this mysterious family conference is about.

[*Awkward silence. Big Mama looks from face to face, then belches slightly and mutters, "Excuse me . . ." She opens an ornamental fan suspended about her throat. A black lace fan to go with her black lace gown, and fans her wilting corsage, sniffing nervously and looking from face to face in the uncomfortable silence as Margaret calls "Brick?" and Brick sings to the moon on the gallery.*]

MARGARET:
Brick, they're gonna tell Big Mama the truth an' she's gonna need you.

BIG MAMA:
I don't know what's wrong here, you all have such long faces! Open that door on the hall and let some air circulate through here, will you please, Gooper?

MAE:
I think we'd better leave that door closed, Big Mama, till after the talk.

MARGARET:
Brick!

BIG MAMA:
Reveren' Tooker, will *you* please open that door?

REVEREND TOOKER:
I sure will, Big Mama.

MAE:
I just didn't think we ought t' take any chance of Big Daddy hearin' a word of this discussion.

BIG MAMA:
I swan! Nothing's going to be said in Big Daddy's house that he caint hear if he want to!

GOOPER:
Well, Big Mama, it's—

[*Mae gives him a quick, hard poke to shut him up. He glares at her fiercely as she circles before him like a burlesque ballerina, raising her skinny bare arms over her head, jangling her bracelets, exclaiming:*]

MAE:
A breeze! A breeze!

REVEREND TOOKER:
I think this house is the coolest house in the Delta.—Did you all know that Halsey Banks's widow put air-conditioning units in the church and rectory at Friar's Point in memory of Halsey?

[*General conversation has resumed; everybody is chatting so that the stage sounds like a bird cage.*]

GOOPER:
Too bad nobody cools your church off for you. I bet you sweat in that pulpit these hot Sundays, Reverend Tooker.

REVEREND TOOKER:
Yes, my vestments are drenched. Last Sunday the gold in my chasuble faded into the purple.

GOOPER:
Reveren', you musta been preachin' hell's fire last Sunday.

MAE [*at the same time to Doctor Baugh*]:
You reckon those vitamin B12 injections are what they're cracked up t' be, Doc Baugh?

DOCTOR BAUGH:
Well, if you want to be stuck with something I guess they're as good to be stuck with as anything else.

BIG MAMA [*at the gallery door*]:
Maggie, Maggie, aren't you comin' with Brick?

MAE [*suddenly and loudly, creating a silence*]:
I have a strange feeling, I have a peculiar feeling!

BIG MAMA [*turning from the gallery*]:
What feeling?

MAE:
That Brick said somethin' he shouldn't of said t' Big Daddy.

BIG MAMA:
Now what on earth could Brick of said t' Big Daddy that he shouldn't say?

GOOPER:
Big Mama, there's somethin'—

MAE:
NOW, WAIT!

[*She rushes up to Big Mama and gives her a quick hug and kiss. Big Mama pushes her impatiently off.*]

DOCTOR BAUGH:
In my day they had what they call the Keeley cure for heavy drinkers.

BIG MAMA:
Shoot!

DOCTOR BAUGH:
But now I understand they just take some kind of tablets.

GOOPER:
They call them "Annie Bust" tablets.

140

BIG MAMA:
Brick don't need to take *nothin'*.

[*Brick and Margaret appear in gallery doors, Big Mama unaware of his presence behind her.*]

That boy is just broken up over Skipper's death. You know how poor Skipper died. They gave him a big, big dose of that sodium amytal stuff at his home and then they called the ambulance and give him another big, big dose of it at the hospital and that and all of the alcohol in his system fo' months an' months just proved too much for his heart . . . I'm scared of needles! I'm more scared of a needle than the knife . . . I think more people have been needled out of this world than—

[*She stops short and wheels about.*]

Oh—here's Brick! My precious baby—

[*She turns upon Brick with short, fat arms extended, at the same time uttering a loud, short sob, which is both comic and touching. Brick smiles and bows slightly, making a burlesque gesture of gallantry for Margaret to pass before him into the room. Then he hobbles on his crutch directly to the liquor cabinet and there is absolute silence, with everybody looking at Brick as everybody has always looked at Brick when he spoke or moved or appeared. One by one he drops ice cubes in his glass, then suddenly, but not quickly, looks back over his shoulder with a wry, charming smile, and says:*]

BRICK:
I'm sorry! Anyone else?

BIG MAMA [*sadly*]:
No, son. I *wish* you wouldn't!

BRICK:

I wish I didn't have to, Big Mama, but I'm still waiting for that click in my head which makes it all smooth out!

BIG MAMA:

Ow, Brick, you—BREAK MY HEART!

MARGARET [*at same time*]:
Brick, go sit with Big Mama!

BIG MAMA:

I just cain't staiiiiii-nnnnnnnd-it . . .

[*She sobs.*]

MAE:

Now that we're all assembled—

GOOPER:

We kin talk . . .

BIG MAMA:

Breaks my heart . . .

MARGARET:

Sit with Big Mama, Brick, and hold her hand.

[*Big Mama sniffs very loudly three times, almost like three drumbeats in the pocket of silence.*]

BRICK:

You do that, Maggie. I'm a restless cripple. I got to stay on my crutch.

[*Brick hobbles to the gallery door; leans there as if waiting.*]

[*Mae sits beside Big Mama, while Gooper moves in front and sits on the end of the couch, facing her. Reverend Tooker moves nervously into the space between them; on*

142

the other side, Doctor Baugh stands looking at nothing in particular and lights a cigar. Margaret turns away.]

BIG MAMA:

Why're you all *surroundin'* me—like this? Why're you all starin' at me like this an' makin' signs at each other?

[*Reverend Tooker steps back startled.*]

MAE:

Calm yourself, Big Mama.

BIG MAMA:

Calm you'self, *you'self*, Sister Woman. How could I calm myself with everyone starin' at me as if big drops of blood had broken out on m'face? What's this all about, annh! What?

[*Gooper coughs and takes a center position.*]

GOOPER:

Now, Doc Baugh.

MAE:

Doc Baugh?

GOOPER:

Big Mama wants to know the complete truth about the report we got from the Ochsner Clinic.

MAE [*eagerly*]:

—on Big Daddy's condition!

GOOPER:

Yais, on Big Daddy's condition, we got to face it.

DOCTOR BAUGH:

Well . . .

BIG MAMA [*terrified, rising*]:

Is there? Something? Something that I? Don't—know?

143

[*In these few words, this startled, very soft, question, Big Mama reviews the history of her forty-five years with Big Daddy, her great, almost embarrassingly true-hearted and simple-minded devotion to Big Daddy, who must have had something Brick has, who made himself loved so much by the "simple expedient" of not loving enough to disturb his charming detachment, also once coupled, like Brick, with virile beauty.*]

[*Big Mama has a dignity at this moment; she almost stops being fat.*]

DOCTOR BAUGH [*after a pause, uncomfortably*]:
Yes?—Well—

BIG MAMA:
I!!!—want to—*knowwwwww . . .*

[*Immediately she thrusts her fist to her mouth as if to deny that statement. Then for some curious reason, she snatches the withered corsage from her breast and hurls it on the floor and steps on it with her short, fat feet.*]

Somebody must be lyin'!—I want to know!

MAE:
Sit down, Big Mama, sit down on this sofa.

MARGARET:
Brick, go sit with Big Mama.

BIG MAMA:
What is it, what is it?

DOCTOR BAUGH:
I never have seen a more thorough examination than Big Daddy Pollitt was given in all my experience with the Ochsner Clinic.

GOOPER:

It's one of the best in the country.

MAE:

It's THE best in the country—bar *none*!

[*For some reason she gives Gooper a violent poke as she goes past him. He slaps at her hand without removing his eyes from his mother's face.*]

DOCTOR BAUGH:

Of course they were ninety-nine and nine-tenths per cent sure before they even started.

BIG MAMA:

Sure of what, sure of what, sure of—*what?*—*what?*

[*She catches her breath in a startled sob. Mae kisses her quickly. She thrusts Mae fiercely away from her, staring at the Doctor.*]

MAE:

Mommy, be a brave girl!

BRICK [*in the doorway, softly*]:

"By the light, by the light, Of the sil-ve-ry mo-oo-n . . ."

GOOPER:

Shut up!—Brick.

BRICK:

Sorry . . .

[*He wanders out on the gallery.*]

DOCTOR BAUGH:

But now, you see, Big Mama, they cut a piece off this growth, a specimen of the tissue and—

BIG MAMA:

Growth? You told Big Daddy—

DOCTOR BAUGH:
Now wait.

BIG MAMA [*fiercely*]:
You told me and Big Daddy there wasn't a thing wrong with
him but—

MAE:
Big Mama, they always—

GOOPER:
Let Doc Baugh talk, will yuh?

BIG MAMA:
—little spastic condition of—

[*Her breath gives out in a sob.*]

DOCTOR BAUGH:
Yes, that's what we told Big Daddy. But we had this bit of
tissue run through the laboratory and I'm sorry to say the test
was positive on it. It's—well—malignant . . .

[*Pause*]

BIG MAMA:
—Cancer?! Cancer?!

[*Doctor Baugh nods gravely. Big Mama gives a long gasping cry.*]

MAE AND GOOPER:
Now, now, now, Big Mama, you had to know . . .

BIG MAMA:
WHY DIDN'T THEY CUT IT OUT OF HIM? HANH?
HANH?

DOCTOR BAUGH:
Involved too much, Big Mama, too many organs affected.

146

MAE:

Big Mama, the liver's affected and so's the kidneys, both! It's gone way past what they call a—

GOOPER:

A surgical risk.

MAE:

—Uh-huh . . .

[*Big Mama draws a breath like a dying gasp.*]

REVEREND TOOKER:

Tch, tch, tch, tch, tch!

DOCTOR BAUGH:

Yes it's gone past the knife.

MAE:

That's why he's turned yellow, Mommy!

BIG MAMA:

Git away from me, git away from me, Mae!

[*She rises abruptly.*]

I want Brick! Where's Brick? Where is my only son?

MAE:

Mama! Did she say "*only* son"?

GOOPER:

What does that make *me*?

MAE:

A sober responsible man with five precious children!—*Six!*

BIG MAMA:

I want Brick to tell me! Brick! Brick!

MARGARET [*rising from her reflections in a corner*]:

Brick was so upset he went back out.

BIG MAMA:
Brick!

MARGARET:
Mama, let *me* tell you!

BIG MAMA:
No, no, leave me alone, you're not my blood!

GOOPER:
Mama, I'm your son! Listen to *me!*

MAE:
Gooper's your son, he's your first-born!

BIG MAMA:
Gooper never liked Daddy.

MAE [*as if terribly shocked*]:
That's not TRUE!

[*There is a pause. The minister coughs and rises.*]

REVEREND TOOKER [*to Mae*]:
I think I'd better slip away at this point.

[*Discreetly*]

Good night, good night, everybody, and God bless you all . . .
on this place . . .

[*He slips out.*]

[*Mae coughs and points at Big Mama.*]
GOOPER:
Well, Big Mama . . .
[*He sighs.*]

BIG MAMA:
It's all a mistake, I know it's just a bad dream.

DOCTOR BAUGH:
We're gonna keep Big Daddy as comfortable as we can.

BIG MAMA:
Yes, it's just a bad dream, that's all it is, it's just an awful dream.

GOOPER:
In my opinion Big Daddy is having some pain but won't admit that he has it.

BIG MAMA:
Just a dream, a bad dream.

DOCTOR BAUGH:
That's what lots of them do, they think if they don't admit they're having the pain they can sort of escape the fact of it.

GOOPER [*with relish*]:
Yes, they get sly about it, they get real sly about it.

MAE:
Gooper and I think—

GOOPER:
Shut up, Mae! Big Mama, I think—Big Daddy ought to be started on morphine.

BIG MAMA:
Nobody's going to give Big Daddy morphine.

DOCTOR BAUGH:
Now, Big Mama, when that pain strikes it's going to strike mighty hard and Big Daddy's going to need the needle to bear it.

BIG MAMA:
I tell you, nobody's going to give him morphine.

149

MAE:

Big Mama, you don't want to see Big Daddy suffer, you know you—

[*Gooper, standing beside her, gives her a savage poke.*]

DOCTOR BAUGH [*placing a package on the table*]:
I'm leaving this stuff here, so if there's a sudden attack you all won't have to send out for it.

MAE:
I know how to give a hypo.

BIG MAMA:
Nobody's gonna give Big Daddy morphine.

GOOPER:
Mae took a course in nursing during the war.

MARGARET:
Somehow I don't think Big Daddy would want Mae to give him a hypo.

MAE:
You think he'd want *you* to do it?

DOCTOR BAUGH:
Well . . .

[*Doctor Baugh rises.*]

GOOPER:
Doctor Baugh is goin'.

DOCTOR BAUGH:
Yes, I got to be goin'. Well, keep your chin up, Big Mama.

GOOPER [*with jocularity*]:
She's gonna keep *both* chins up, aren't you, Big Mama?

[*Big Mama sobs.*]

Now stop that, Big Mama.

GOOPER [*at the door with Doctor Baugh*]:
Well, Doc, we sure do appreciate all you done. I'm telling you,
we're surely obligated to you for—

[*Doctor Baugh has gone out without a glance at him.*]

—I guess that doctor has got a lot on his mind but it wouldn't
hurt him to act a little more human . . .

[*Big Mama sobs.*]

Now be a brave girl, Mommy.

BIG MAMA:
It's not true, I know that it's just not true!

GOOPER:
Mama, those tests are infallible!

BIG MAMA:
Why are you so determined to see your father daid?

MAE:
Big Mama!

MARGARET [*gently*]:
I know what Big Mama means.

MAE [*fiercely*]:
Oh, do you?

MARGARET [*quietly and very sadly*]:
Yes, I think I do.

MAE:
For a newcomer in the family you sure do show a lot of understanding.

MARGARET:
Understanding is needed on this place.

MAE:

I guess you must have needed a lot of it in your family, Maggie, with your father's liquor problem and now you've got Brick with his!

MARGARET:

Brick does not have a liquor problem at all. Brick is devoted to Big Daddy. This thing is a terrible strain on him.

BIG MAMA:

Brick is Big Daddy's boy, but he drinks too much and it worries me and Big Daddy, and, Margaret, you've got to co-operate with us, you've got to co-operate with Big Daddy and me in getting Brick straightened out. Because it will break Big Daddy's heart if Brick don't pull himself together and take hold of things.

MAE:

Take hold of *what* things, Big Mama?

BIG MAMA:

The place.

[*There is a quick violent look between Mae and Gooper.*]

GOOPER:

Big Mama, you've had a shock.

MAE:

Yais, we've all had a shock, but . . .

GOOPER:

Let's be realistic—

MAE:

—Big Daddy would never, would *never*, be foolish enough to—

GOOPER:

—put this place in irresponsible hands!

BIG MAMA:

Big Daddy ain't going to leave the place in anybody's hands; Big Daddy is *not* going to die. I want you to get that in your heads, all of you!

MAE:

Mommy, Mommy, Big Mama, we're just as hopeful an' optimistic as you are about Big Daddy's prospects, we have faith in *prayer*—but nevertheless there are certain matters that have to be discussed an' dealt with, because otherwise—

GOOPER:

Eventualities have to be considered and now's the time . . . Mae, will you please get my brief case out of our room?

MAE:

Yes, honey.

[*She rises and goes out through the hall door.*]

GOOPER [*standing over Big Mama*]:

Now, Big Mom. What you said just now was not at all true and you know it. I've always loved Big Daddy in my own quiet way. I never made a show of it, and I know that Big Daddy has always been fond of me in a quiet way, too, and he never made a show of it neither.

[*Mae returns with Gooper's brief case.*]

MAE:

Here's your brief case, Gooper, honey.

GOOPER [*handing the brief case back to her*]:

Thank you . . . Of cou'se, my relationship with Big Daddy is different from Brick's.

MAE:

You're eight years older'n Brick an' always had t' carry a bigger load of th' responsibilities than Brick ever had t' carry.

153

He never carried a thing in his life but a football or a high-ball.

GOOPER:
Mae, will y' let me talk, please?

MAE:
Yes, honey.

GOOPER:
Now, a twenty-eight-thousand-acre plantation's a mighty big thing t' run.

MAE:
Almost singlehanded.

[*Margaret has gone out onto the gallery and can be heard calling softly to Brick.*]

BIG MAMA:
You never had to run this place! What are you talking about? As if Big Daddy was dead and in his grave, you had to run it? Why, you just helped him out with a few business details and had your law practice at the same time in Memphis!

MAE:
Oh, Mommy, Mommy, Big Mommy! Let's be fair!

MARGARET:
Brick!

MAE:
Why, Gooper has given himself body and soul to keeping this place up for the past five years since Big Daddy's health started failing.

MARGARET:
Brick!

MAE:
Gooper won't say it, Gooper never thought of it as a duty, he just did it. And what did Brick do? Brick kept living in his past glory at college! Still a football player at twenty-seven!

MARGARET [*returning alone*]:
Who are you talking about now? Brick? A football player? He isn't a football player and you know it. Brick is a sports announcer on T.V. and one of the best-known ones in the country!

MAE:
I'm talking about what he was.

MARGARET:
Well, I wish you would just stop talking about my husband.

GOOPER:
I've got a right to discuss my brother with other members of MY OWN family, which don't include *you*. Why don't you go out there and drink with Brick?

MARGARET:
I've never seen such malice toward a brother.

GOOPER:
How about his for me? Why, he can't stand to be in the same room with me!

MARGARET:
This is a deliberate campaign of vilification for the most disgusting and sordid reason on earth, and I know what it is! It's *avarice, avarice, greed, greed!*

BIG MAMA:
Oh, I'll scream! I will scream in a moment unless this stops!

[*Gooper has stalked up to Margaret with clenched fists at his sides as if he would strike her. Mae distorts her face again into a hideous grimace behind Margaret's back.*]

155

BIG MAMA [*sobs*]:
Margaret. Child. Come here. Sit next to Big Mama.

MARGARET:
Precious Mommy. I'm sorry, I'm sorry, I—!

[*She bends her long graceful neck to press her forehead to Big Mama's bulging shoulder under its black chiffon.*]

MAE:
How beautiful, how touching, this display of devotion! Do you know why she's childless? She's childless because that big beautiful athlete husband of hers won't go to bed with her!

GOOPER:
You jest won't let me do this in a nice way, will yah? Aw right—I don't give a goddam if Big Daddy likes me or don't like me or did or never did or will or will never! I'm just appealing to a sense of common decency and fair play. I'll tell you the truth. I've resented Big Daddy's partiality to Brick ever since Brick was born, and the way I've been treated like I was just barely good enough to spit on and sometimes not even good enough for that. Big Daddy is dying of cancer, and it's spread all through him and it's attacked all his vital organs including the kidneys and right now he is sinking into uremia, and you all know what uremia is, it's poisoning of the whole system due to the failure of the body to eliminate its poisons.

MARGARET [*to herself, downstage, hissingly*]:
Poisons, poisons! Venomous thoughts and words! In hearts and minds!—That's poisons!

GOOPER [*overlapping her*]:
I am asking for a square deal, and, by God, I expect to get one. But if I don't get one, if there's any peculiar shenanigans going on around here behind my back, well, I'm not a corpo-

ration lawyer for nothing, I know how to protect my own interests.

[*Brick enters from the gallery with a tranquil, blurred smile, carrying an empty glass with him.*]

BRICK:
Storm coming up.

GOOPER:
Oh! A late arrival!

MAE:
Behold the conquering hero comes!

GOOPER:
The̅ fabulous Brick Pollitt! Remember him?—Who could forget him!

MAE:
He looks like he's been injured in a game!

GOOPER:
Yep, I'm afraid you'll have to warm the bench at the Sugar Bowl this year, Brick!

[*Mae laughs shrilly.*]

Or was it the Rose Bowl that he made that famous run in?—

[*Thunder*]

MAE:
The punch bowl, honey. It was in the punch bowl, the cut-glass punch bowl!

GOOPER:
Oh, that's right, I'm getting the bowls mixed up!

MARGARET:
Why don't you stop venting your malice and envy on a sick boy?

157

BIG MAMA:
Now you two hush, I mean it, hush, all of you, hush!

DAISY, SOOKEY:
Storm! Storm comin'! Storm! Storm!

LACEY:
Brightie, close them shutters.

GOOPER:
Lacey, put the top up on my Cadillac, will yuh?

LACEY:
Yes, suh, Mistah Pollitt!

GOOPER [*at the same time*]:
Big Mama, you know it's necessary for me t' go back to Memphis in th' mornin' t' represent the Parker estate in a lawsuit.

[*Mae sits on the bed and arranges papers she has taken from the brief case.*]

BIG MAMA:
Is it, Gooper?

MAE:
Yaiss.

GOOPER:
That's why I'm forced to—to bring up a problem that—

MAE:
Somethin' that's too important t' be put off!

GOOPER:
If Brick was sober, he ought to be in on this.

MARGARET:
Brick is present; we're present.

158

GOOPER:
Well, good. I will now give you this outline my partner, Tom Bullitt, an' me have drawn up—a sort of dummy—trusteeship.

MARGARET:
Oh, that's it! You'll be in charge an' dole out remittances, will you?

GOOPER:
This we did as soon as we got the report on Big Daddy from th' Ochsner Laboratories. We did this thing, I mean we drew up this dummy outline with the advice and assistance of the Chairman of the Boa'd of Directors of th' Southern Plantahs Bank and Trust Company in Memphis, C. C. Bellowes, a man who handles estates for all th' prominent fam'lies in West Tennessee and th' Delta.

BIG MAMA:
Gooper?

GOOPER [*crouching in front of Big Mama*]:
Now this is not—not final, or anything like it. This is just a preliminary outline. But it does provide a basis—a design—a—possible, feasible—*plan!*

MARGARET:
Yes, I'll bet it's a plan.

[*Thunder*]

MAE:
It's a plan to protect the biggest estate in the Delta from irresponsibility an'—

BIG MAMA:
Now you listen to me, all of you, you listen here! They's not goin' to be any more catty talk in my house! And Gooper,

you put that away before I grab it out of your hand and tear it right up! I don't know what the hell's in it, and I don't want to know what the hell's in it. I'm talkin' in Big Daddy's language now; I'm his *wife*, not his *widow*, I'm still his *wife!* And I'm talkin' to you in his language an'—

GOOPER:
Big Mama, what I have here is —

MAE [*at the same time*]:
Gooper explained that it's just a plan . . .

BIG MAMA:
I don't care what you got there. Just put it back where it came from, an' don't let me see it again, not even the outside of the envelope of it! Is that understood? Basis! Plan! Preliminary! Design! I say—what is it Big Daddy always says when he's disgusted?

BRICK [*from the bar*]:
Big Daddy says "crap" when he's disgusted.

BIG MAMA [*rising*]:
That's right—CRAP! I say CRAP too, like Big Daddy!

[*Thunder*]

MAE:
Coarse language doesn't seem called for in this—

GOOPER:
Somethin' in me is *deeply outraged* by hearin' you talk like this.

BIG MAMA:
Nobody's goin' to take nothin'!—till Big Daddy lets go of it —maybe, just possibly, not—not even then! No, not even then!

[*Thunder*]

MAE:

Sookey, hurry up an' git that po'ch furniture covahed; want th' paint to come off?

GOOPER:

Lacey, put mah car away!

LACEY:

Caint, Mistah Pollitt, you got the keys!

GOOPER:

Naw, you got 'em, man. Where th' keys to th' car, honey?

MAE:

You got 'em in your pocket!

BRICK:

"You can always hear me singin' this song, Show me the way to go home."

[Thunder distantly]

BIG MAMA:

Brick! Come here, Brick, I need you. Tonight Brick looks like he used to look when he was a little boy, just like he did when he played wild games and used to come home when I hollered myself hoarse for him, all sweaty and pink cheeked and sleepy, with his—red curls shining . . .

[Brick draws aside as he does from all physical contact and continues the song in a whisper, opening the ice bucket and dropping in the ice cubes one by one as if he were mixing some important chemical formula.]

[Distant thunder.]

Time goes by so fast. Nothin' can outrun it. Death commences too early—almost before you're half acquainted with life— you meet the other . . . Oh, you know we just got to love each

161

other an' stay together, all of us, just as close as we can, especially now that such a *black* thing has come and moved into this place without invitation.

[*Awkwardly embracing Brick, she presses her head to his shoulder.*]

[*A dog howls off stage.*]

Oh, Brick, son of Big Daddy, Big Daddy does so love you. Y'know what would be his fondest dream come true? If before he passed on, if Big Daddy has to pass on...

[*A dog howls.*]

...you give him a child of yours, a grandson as much like his son as his son is like Big Daddy...

MARGARET:
I know that's Big Daddy's dream.

BIG MAMA:
That's his dream.

MAE:
Such a pity that Maggie and Brick can't oblige.

BIG DADDY [*off down stage right on the gallery*]:
Looks like the wind was takin' liberties with this place.

SERVANT [*off stage*]:
Yes, sir, Mr. Pollitt.

MARGARET [*crossing to the right door*]:
Big Daddy's on the gall'ry.

[*Big Mama has turned toward the hall door at the sound of Big Daddy's voice on the gallery.*]

BIG MAMA:
I can't stay here. He'll see somethin' in my eyes.

[*Big Daddy enters the room from up stage right.*]

BIG DADDY:
Can I come in?

[*He puts his cigar in an ash tray.*]

MARGARET:
Did the storm wake you up, Big Daddy?

BIG DADDY:
Which stawm are you talkin' about—th' one outside or th' hullballoo in here?

[*Gooper squeezes past Big Daddy.*]

GOOPER:
'Scuse me.

Mae tries to squeeze past Big Daddy to join Gooper, but Big Daddy puts his arm firmly around her.]

BIG DADDY:
I heard some mighty loud talk. Sounded like somethin' important was bein' discussed. What was the powwow about?

MAE [*flustered*]:
Why—nothin', Big Daddy . . .

BIG DADDY [*crossing to extreme left center, taking Mae with him*]:
What is that pregnant-lookin' envelope you're puttin' back in your brief case, Gooper?

GOOPER [*at the foot of the bed, caught, as he stuffs papers into envelope*]:
That? Nothin,' suh—nothin' much of anythin' at all . . .

BIG DADDY:
Nothin'? It looks like a whole lot of nothin'!

[*He turns up stage to the group.*]

You all know th' story about th' young married couple—

GOOPER:
Yes, sir!

BIG DADDY:
Hello, Brick—

BRICK:
Hello, Big Daddy.

[*The group is arranged in a semicircle above Big Daddy, Margaret at the extreme right, then Mae and Gooper, then Big Mama, with Brick at the left.*]

BIG DADDY:
Young married couple took Junior out to th' zoo one Sunday, inspected all of God's creatures in their cages, with satisfaction.

GOOPER:
Satisfaction.

BIG DADDY [*crossing to up stage center, facing front*]:
This afternoon was a warm afternoon in spring an' that ole elephant had somethin' else on his mind which was bigger'n peanuts. You know this story, Brick?

[*Gooper nods.*]

BRICK:
No, sir, I don't know it.

BIG DADDY:
Y'see, in th' cage adjoinin' they was a young female elephant in heat!

BIG MAMA [*at Big Daddy's shoulder*]:
Oh, Big Daddy!

164

BIG DADDY:

What's the matter, preacher's gone, ain't he? All right. That female elephant in the next cage was permeatin' the atmosphere about her with a powerful and excitin' odor of female fertility! Huh! Ain't that a nice way to put it, Brick?

BRICK:

Yes, sir, nothin' wrong with it.

BIG DADDY:

Brick says th's nothin' wrong with it!

BIG MAMA:

Oh, Big Daddy!

BIG DADDY [*crossing to down stage center*]:

So this ole bull elephant still had a couple of fornications left in him. He reared back his trunk an' got a whiff of that elephant lady next door!—began to paw at the dirt in his cage an' butt his head against the separatin' partition and, first thing y'know, there was a conspicuous change in his *profile*— very *conspicuous!* Ain't I tellin' this story in decent language, Brick?

BRICK:

Yes, sir, too fuckin' decent!

BIG DADDY:

So, the little boy pointed at it and said, "What's that?" His mama said, "Oh, that's—nothin'!"—His papa said, "She's spoiled!"

[*Big Daddy crosses to Brick at left.*]

You didn't laugh at that story, Brick.

[*Big Mama crosses to down stage right crying. Margaret goes to her. Mae and Gooper hold up stage right center.*]

165

BRICK:

No, sir, I didn't laugh at that story.

BIG DADDY:

What is the smell in this room? Don't you notice it, Brick? Don't you notice a powerful and obnoxious odor of mendacity in this room?

BRICK:

Yes, sir, I think I do, sir.

GOOPER:

Mae, Mae . . .

BIG DADDY:

There is nothing more powerful. Is there, Brick?

BRICK:

No, sir. No, sir, there isn't, an' nothin' more obnoxious.

BIG DADDY:

Brick agrees with me. The odor of mendacity is a powerful and obnoxious odor an' the stawm hasn't blown it away from this room yet. You notice it, Gooper?

GOOPER:

What, sir?

BIG DADDY:

How about you, Sister Woman? You notice the unpleasant odor of mendacity in this room?

MAE:

Why, Big Daddy, I don't even know what that is.

BIG DADDY:

You can smell it. Hell it smells like death!

[*Big Mama sobs. Big Daddy looks toward her.*]

What's wrong with that fat woman over there, loaded with diamonds? Hey, what's-you-name, what's the matter with you?

MARGARET [*crossing toward Big Daddy*]:
She had a slight dizzy spell, Big Daddy.

BIG DADDY:
You better watch that, Big Mama. A stroke is a bad way to go.

MARGARET [*crossing to Big Daddy at center*]:
Oh, Brick, Big Daddy has on your birthday present to him, Brick, he has on your cashmere robe, the softest material I have ever felt.

BIG DADDY:
Yeah, this is my soft birthday, Maggie... Not my gold or my silver birthday, but my soft birthday, everything's got to be soft for Big Daddy on this soft birthday.

[*Maggie kneels before Big Daddy at center.*]

MARGARET:
Big Daddy's got on his Chinese slippers that I gave him, Brick. Big Daddy, I haven't given you my big present yet, but now I will, now's the time for me to present it to you! I have an announcement to make!

MAE:
What? What kind of announcement?

GOOPER:
A sports announcement, Maggie?

MARGARET:
Announcement of life beginning! A child is coming, sired by Brick, and out of Maggie the Cat! I have Brick's child in my body, an' that's my birthday present to Big Daddy on this birthday!

167

[*Big Daddy looks at Brick who crosses behind Big Daddy to down stage portal, left.*]

BIG DADDY:
Get up, girl, get up off your knees, girl.

[*Big Daddy helps Margaret to rise. He crosses above her, to her right, bites off the end of a fresh cigar, taken from his bathrobe pocket, as he studies Margaret.*]

Uh-huh, this girl has life in her body, that's no lie!

BIG MAMA:
BIG DADDY'S DREAM COME TRUE!

BRICK:
JESUS!

BIG DADDY [*crossing right below wicker stand*]:
Gooper, I want my lawyer in the mornin'.

BRICK:
Where are you goin', Big Daddy?

BIG DADDY:
Son, I'm goin' up on the roof, to the belvedere on th' roof to look over my kingdom before I give up my kingdom— twenty-eight thousand acres of th' richest land this side of the valley Nile!

[*He exits through right doors, and down right on the gallery.*]

BIG MAMA [*following*]:
Sweetheart, sweetheart, sweetheart—can I come with you?

[*She exits down stage right.*]

[*Margaret is down stage center in the mirror area. Mae has joined Gooper and she gives him a fierce poke, making a low hissing sound and a grimace of fury.*]

GOOPER [*pushing her aside*]:
Brick, could you possibly spare me one small shot of that liquor?

BRICK:
Why, help yourself, Gooper boy.

GOOPER:
I will.

MAE [*shrilly*]:
Of course we know that this is—a lie.

GOOPER:
Be still, Mae.

MAE:
I won't be still! I know she's made this up!

GOOPER:
Goddam it, I said shut up!

MARGARET:
Gracious! I didn't know that my little announcement was going to provoke such a storm!

MAE:
That woman isn't *pregnant!*

GOOPER:
Who said she was?

MAE:
She did.

GOOPER:
The doctor didn't. Doc Baugh didn't.

MARGARET:
I haven't gone to Doc Baugh.

169

GOOPER:
Then who'd you go to, Maggie?

MARGARET:
One of the best gynecologists in the South.

GOOPER:
Uh huh, uh huh!—I see . . .

[*He takes out a pencil and notebook.*]

—May we have his name, please?

MARGARET:
No, you may not, Mister Prosecuting Attorney!

MAE:
He doesn't have any name, he doesn't exist!

MARGARET:
Oh, he exists all right, and so does my child, Brick's baby!

MAE:
You can't conceive a child by a man that won't sleep with you
unless you think you're—

[*Brick has turned on the phonograph. A scat song cuts
Mae's speech.*]

GOOPER:
Turn that off!

MAE:
We know it's a lie because we hear you in here; he won't
sleep with you, we hear you! So don't imagine you're going to
put a trick over on us, to fool a dying man with a—

[*A long drawn cry of agony and rage fills the house.
Margaret turns the phonograph down to a whisper. The
cry is repeated.*]

170

MAE:

Did you hear that, Gooper, did you hear that?

GOOPER:

Sounds like the pain has struck.

GOOPER:

Come along and leave these lovebirds together in their nest!

[*He goes out first. Mae follows but turns at the door, contorting her face and hissing at Margaret.*]

MAE:

Liar!

[*She slams the door.*]

[*Margaret exhales with relief and moves a little unsteadily to catch hold of Brick's arm.*]

MARGARET:

Thank you for—keeping still . . .

BRICK:

O.K., Maggie.

MARGARET:

It was gallant of you to save my face!

[*He now pours down three shots in quick succession and stands waiting, silent. All at once he turns with a smile and says:*]

BRICK:

There!

MARGARET:

What?

BRICK:

The *click* . . .

171

[*His gratitude seems almost infinite as he hobbles out on the gallery with a drink. We hear his crutch as he swings out of sight. Then, at some distance, he begins singing to himself a peaceful song. Margaret holds the big pillow forlornly as if it were her only companion, for a few moments, then throws it on the bed. She rushes to the liquor cabinet, gathers all the bottles in her arms, turns about undecidedly, then runs out of the room with them, leaving the door ajar on the dim yellow hall. Brick is heard hobbling back along the gallery, singing his peaceful song. He comes back in, sees the pillow on the bed, laughs lightly, sadly, picks it up. He has it under his arm as Margaret returns to the room. Margaret softly shuts the door and leans against it, smiling softly at Brick.*]

MARGARET:

Brick, I used to think that you were stronger than me and I didn't want to be overpowered by you. But now, since you've taken to liquor—you know what?—I guess it's bad, but now I'm stronger than you and I can love you more truly! Don't move that pillow. I'll move it right back if you do!—Brick?

[*She turns out all the lamps but a single rose-silk-shaded one by the bed.*]

I really have been to a doctor and I know what to do and—Brick?—this is my time by the calendar to conceive?

BRICK:

Yes, I understand, Maggie. But how are you going to conceive a child by a man in love with his liquor?

MARGARET:

By locking his liquor up and making him satisfy my desire before I unlock it!

BRICK:

Is that what you've done, Maggie?

MARGARET:

Look and see. That cabinet's mighty empty compared to before!

BRICK:

Well, I'll be a son of a—

[He reaches for his crutch but she beats him to it and rushes out on the gallery, hurls the crutch over the rail and comes back in, panting.]

MARGARET:

And so tonight we're going to make the lie true, and when that's done, I'll bring the liquor back here and we'll get drunk together, here, tonight, in this place that death has come into...—What do you say?

BRICK:

I don't say anything. I guess there's nothing to say.

MARGARET:

Oh, you weak people, you weak, beautiful people!—who give up with such grace. What you want is someone to—

[She turns out the rose-silk lamp.]

—take hold of you.—Gently, gently with love hand your life back to you, like somethin' gold you let go of. I *do* love you, Brick, I *do!*

BRICK *[smiling with charming sadness]*:

Wouldn't it be funny if that was true?

THE END

SWINGING A CAT

by Brian Parker

Cat on a Hot Tin Roof was a favorite with Fidel Castro who greeted Tennessee Williams at their first meeting with "Oh, that Cat!" And according to his *Memoirs*, it was also Williams' own favorite among his plays, for two reasons: he was proud of its tight classical unity, with continuous action in a single location occupying only the same time as its staging, and also of what he calls "a kind of crude eloquence of expression in Big Daddy that I have managed to give no other character of my creation."

After try-outs in Philadelphia, *Cat* opened on Broadway on March 24, 1955 with Elia Kazan directing, Jo Mielziner designing, Ben Gazzara as Brick, Barbara Bel Geddes as Maggie (to Williams' annoyance—he thought her voice too unmusical for the role), Burl Ives as an unforgettable Big Daddy, and Mildred Dunnock as Big Mama. It ran for 694 performances, and won a Donaldson Award, the Drama Critics Circle Award, and Williams' second Pulitzer Prize; and three years later it was made into a commercially successful film for MGM by Richard Brooks, with Elizabeth Taylor as Maggie the Cat and Paul Newman as Brick. Since then it has been continuously revived, with its most recent incarnation—literally as I write these words—at the Kennedy Center in Washington under the direction of Mark Lamos.

Like all imaginative writers, Tennessee Williams synthesized details from his personal experience to create fictional characters, so biographical commentators have found many real-life "models" for people in the play. Williams' friend Maria St. Just, for instance, claimed that she was the prototype for Maggie ("no-neck monsters" was certainly one of her jokes), but the nickname "Maggie the Cat," according to Williams' biographer Lyle Leverich, derives from Margaret Lewis Powell, an acquaintance made in Macon, Georgia, in the summer of 1942. And that same summer Williams also met Jordan Massie Sr., the father of one of his Macon friends, who was called "Big Daddy" because of his size (though the title is common in the South), used the phrase "nervous as a cat on a hot tin roof," and told stories about plantation life "on the richest land this side of the Valley Nile." On the other hand, Big Daddy also has resemblances to Williams' rambunctious father; and one of the early manuscripts of the play includes a clipping from a 1921 newspaper about a Williams neighbor G.D. Perry, his substantial wife, and their nine bulky children. Like Big Daddy, Perry rose from manager to owner of a 7,500-acre plantation close to Clarksdale, Mississippi, where Williams was raised, and was a friend of the playwright's grandfather, the Reverend Walter Dakin.

Real life models remain problematic, then, but the main literary source for *Cat* was undoubtedly the short story called *Three Players of a Summer Game* written by Williams in 1952. In this story an alcoholic ex-athlete called Brick Pollitt, estranged from his bossy wife, has an affair with the widow of a young doctor whose musical voice is mocked by bratty children, drunkenly falls over while playing croquet with her and her plump, foolish little daughter, and is eventually repossessed by his wife and driven around town like the captive in a Roman triumph. Some of the manuscript drafts of this story have "background material" that fills in even more details of the play, including the names "Gooper," Big Mama," and

"Little Mama," and the phrase "eight thousand acres of the richest, darkest soil this side of the valley of the Nile." There is no Skipper character this early, however (though in one draft Brick makes advances to his mulatto chauffeur).

Williams' friend Donald Windham claims that some of *Cat*'s denunciations of "mendacity" were inserted into his own play *The Starless Air*, when Williams directed it as early as May 1953, and Williams apparently began drafting the full-length *Cat* in Rome that summer but was depressed because he could not find a shape for it. In March 1954 he sent a letter to his agent, Audrey Wood, informing her that he was putting together a "short-long play based on the characters in 'Three Players' which I started last summer in Rome, but don't expect that till you see it as I might not like it when I read it aloud." This was almost certainly a revision subtitled "*A Place of Stone*" that has an epigraph from a poem by W.B. Yeats (emphasizing Maggie's tenacity), which Williams later replaced with lines from Dylan Thomas's famous poem to his dying father, "Do not go gentle into that good night." The *Place of Stone* revision has whole sections dealing with the doctor dying from cancer and his desperate wife, derived from the short story.

In two fragmentary copies of this *Place of Stone* version (one at the University of Texas, the other at Harvard) there are green ink annotations by Elia Kazan, deleting the Yeats epigraph, suggesting "Dylan Thomas reading" as a stylistic model, advising that Big Daddy speak directly to the audience, and sketching a set angled into the auditorium to encourage such direct addresses—thus emphasizing the non-realistic almost musical structure of the play, in which Maggie dominates Act One with what is practically an aria, Act Two focuses on a duet between Brick and Big Daddy, and Act Three is finally an ensemble. This sketch is very unlike Williams' own set description but is the one that Jo Mielziner would eventually follow in the first production. Kazan also repeatedly stresses his admiration for Maggie and follows Williams' emending pencil in deleting all passages dealing with the dying doctor and his wife. However, the removal of these passages left the text too short for a full-length play, so Audrey Wood pressed Williams to add another act, while he repeatedly insisted that its three-part arrangement was "the tightest structure of anything I have done" and suggested that one of his one-acts might be used as a curtain raiser instead.

Since there is a complete lack of data about *Cat* in the Kazan archives at Wesleyan University in Connecticut, it is not clear exactly when Kazan became involved in the production. Williams had the habit of sending work-in-progress to Kazan for comment (and in hopes of interesting him enough to direct) and the annotations to the *Place of Stone* version suggest quite an early input. Kazan did not come officially onboard, however, till October 1954, and immediately began to press for rewrites that Williams wrote Maria St. Just were keeping him as busy as a "cat on a hot tin roof." After the disappointing box-office of his two previous plays, *The Rose Tattoo* and *Camino Real*, Williams desperately needed another success and was anxious to obtain Kazan as director; so the changes were made (mostly in Act Three) but were resented by the author. And this was to cause trouble and confusion in the future.

When New Directions first published *Cat* in 1955, shortly after its Broadway opening, the volume included two versions of Act Three—one which Williams referred to as "*Cat* Number One" (which first reached the stage in 1958 in London), the other the "Broadway Version"—with a "Note of Explanation" by Williams between them, describing the major changes Kazan had asked for and his own attitude toward them. (*The Theatre of Tennessee Williams, Volume III* includes both versions and Williams' "Note.") The changes were three in number. According to Williams, Kazan "felt that Big Daddy was too vivid and important a character to disappear from the play except as an offstage cry after the second act curtain." Secondly, Kazan felt that the character of Brick should undergo a change after his altercation with his father in Act Two. And, thirdly, Kazan wanted the character of Maggie to be "more clearly sympathetic to the audience." Williams had no difficulty with the last of these suggestions, but did not want Big Daddy to reappear in Act Three and felt that "the moral paralysis of Brick was a root thing in his tragedy, and to show a dramatic progression would obscure the meaning of the tragedy in him and because I don't believe that a conversion, however revelatory, ever effects so immediate a change in the heart or even conduct of a person in Brick's state of spiritual disrepair." A recurrent disagreement between Williams and Kazan, in fact, was that Kazan, true to what Williams calls his "lefty" training in the Group Theatre, considered that events should be shown to alter character, whereas Williams believed that they could only reveal what was basic and unchanging in a personality.

Kazan's response to this edition was that he had merely made suggestions, not delivered ultimatums, and that Williams' changes had be made for box-office reasons—an argument that Williams had already partly conceded at the end of his "Note": "The reception of the playing-script has more than justified, in my opinion, the adjustments made [in response to Kazan's] influence. A failure reaches fewer people, and touches fewer, than does a play that succeeds." In his autobiography, *Elia Kazan: A Life*, however, Kazan also admits that by this stage of his career he had decided no longer to serve the playwrights he directed but to make them contributors to his own artistic vision. When newspapers tried to exploit this disagreement, both men hastened to reassert their admiration and affection for each other, which were real enough despite their very different temperaments.

As his "Note of Explanation" suggests, Williams had no difficulty in making Maggie more attractive for the "Broadway Version." He dropped some of her catty exchanges with her sister-in-law, Mae; had her support and show warm physical affection for Big Mama, emphasizing their parallel situations; and also established a strong attraction between Maggie and Big Daddy. With Brick, however, and particularly with Big Daddy, Williams found himself in difficulties.

Brick was shown to be changed by his encounter with Big Daddy by having him encourage his father's mildy smutty elephant story (though this was changed during the run); by having him defend Maggie against Mae's sneer that she cannot possibly be pregnant because Brick won't sleep with her anymore (instead of remaining noncommittally silent); and by having him respond to Maggie's destruction of his liquor cache by saying, "Maggie, I admire you" and surrendering without further protest to her invitation to bed, instead of replying to her avowals of love by repeating his father's indifferent response earlier to Big Mama, "Wouldn't it be funny if that was true?" This supported Williams' insistence that Brick was heterosexual, not a closeted gay man; but it removed the aura of ambiguity that had been created by his passivity and stubborn silences—that core of mystery that Williams thought indispensable for full characterization. He also feared the denouement might be sentimentally interpreted as comparable to the end of Robert Anderson's *Tea and Sympathy*, with which Kazan had just had a Broadway success. The guilt for which

Brick is punishing both himself and Maggie is not necessarily homosexual repression nor even homophobia, but the lack of compassion that made him hang up on Skipper's drunken confession (like Blanche's similar "cruelty" to Allan Grey in *Streetcar*): "*You! —*dug the grave of your friend and kicked him into it!" accuses Big Daddy, "before you'd face the truth with him." The click of that disconnection is echoed in the self-annihilating "click" that Brick drinks for, killing himself with liquor like his friend.

The return of Big Daddy presented even more problems. "I had to violate my own intuition by having Big Daddy reenter the stage in Act Three," writes Williams in his *Memoirs*; "I saw nothing for him to do in the act when he reentered and I did not think it was dramatically proper that he should reenter." Influenced probably by the line "And you, my father, there on the sad height" of the Dylan Thomas epigraph, Williams at first wrote drafts in which Big Daddy mounts to a belvedere on the roof to oversee and comment on the family struggle below, before succumbing to the pain of cancer just as Maggie turns out her bedroom light—and in one strange fragment he even shoots arrows from the belvedere with Maggie's prize-winning bow at anyone venturing onto the balconies below. The final paragraph of this belvedere draft sums up what Williams saw to be his problem:

> I don't think a soft, or sentimental ending, can do anything but injury to the play which says only one affirmative thing about "Man's Fate": that he has it still in his power not to squeal like a pig but to keep a tight mouth about it...and also that love is possible: not *proven* or *disproven*, but possible. (Williams' own ellipsis and italics.)

Eventually Williams had Big Daddy come back on stage to tell his mildly smutty joke about the old bull elephant with an erection. And immediately after, when Maggie kneeling before him lies that she is pregnant, this story was dramatized by having Big Daddy raise her and lubriciously stroke the silk pajamas over her belly before affirming "This girl has life in her body, that's no lie." Though photographs survive of this business in the Philadelphia tryout, it was cut before the New York opening (Burl Ives' acting script even has a note reminding himself only to stare), which left the elephant story irrelevantly freestanding and, as Audrey Wood complained, a very unlikely joke to occur to a man who has just learned painfully that he is dying of cancer. Williams claimed never to have liked the elephant joke anyway, and took advantage of an early visit from the New York Licensing Commission (and Kazan's absence in Europe) to remove it, replacing it with an exchange between Big Daddy and Brick about the "odor of mendacity" that reprises the beginning of their conversation in Act Two.

It is this "mendacity" version of Act Three that is printed in the 1958 Dramatists Play Service edition, along with a lot of stage business elaborated by Kazan (also, more partially, recorded in the "Broadway Version" Act Three). The Dramatists Play Service version includes a violent thunderstorm in Act Three, the symbolic significance of which is emphasized a little heavy-handedly by Big Daddy's demand on reentering, "What stawm are you talkin' about, th' one outside or th' hullaballou in here?" Extra servants and children are added, with servants beginning the play instead of Maggie; there are off-stage sounds of a croquet game, dogs barking, birthday fireworks, and "plantation-type" songs by the Negro field hands; and chants and irritating extra business are invented for Gooper's "no-neck monsters." These provide the wraparound social context typical of a Kazan production, instead of Williams' intense focus on what he calls (in an Act Two stage direction) "that cloudy, flickering, evanescent—fiercely charged! —interplay of live human beings in the thundercloud of a common crisis." Kazan literalized Williams' metaphor with actual thunder and lightning, and this externality was taken further in Richard Brooks' 1958 movie, which also "opened up" Williams' concentration on the bedroom to other locales and emphasized the reconciliation of Maggie and Brick even more sentimentally than Kazan. Williams did not like this film version at all.

To understand why Williams allowed these many variants, it is necessary to remember not only his concern to get his work out to as wide an audience as possible but also his extraordinary method of composition. He dashed off draft after draft at high speed without prior planning in order to try to tap subconscious levels of experience. So, he told Kazan about *Cat*'s predecessor, *The Rose Tattoo*:

> I have this terrific creative will in me tearing me and fighting to get out and from its own fury creating its own block, so I work more or less blindly: the good values are from the subconscious, so often when I am finished I have no idea what I have done, what is good or bad in it.

The advantage of such a headlong method of composition is that it can tap great originality and complexity of feeling; its disadvantage, as Williams admits, is that the writer does not always know what the best parts of his work are, and relies too heavily on others to guide him. It creates great problems, but also opportunities, for collation.

A final text of *Cat*, produced during Williams' lifetime and reprinted in the present volume, was prepared for a production directed by Michael Kahn at the American Shakespeare Theater in Stratford, Connecticut, in July 1974, then transferred (with revisions) to the ANTA theater in New York. This production was notable for an electrifying performance by Elizabeth Ashley as Maggie that Williams praised as perfect (see Ashley's autobiography, *Actress*, 1978). It restored Williams' original ideas about stage design, with the bedroom opening up to the immensity of a "galactic" sky, and discarded most, though not all, of Kazan's elaborations of staging. And its version of Act Three is an intriguing amalgam of "Cat Number One" and the "Broadway Version." Big Daddy returns in Act Three to tell his elephant joke and *also* its replacement, the "odor of mendacity" exchange (though the latter was removed for the transition to New York), but we also hear his bellows of agony offstage and in a film record of the production (though it was dropped from the printed text) Big Mama rushes in for the hypodermic syringe, as in "Cat Number One." The Brick-Maggie relationship is kept enigmatic as originally, with Brick not denying Mae's sneer that he no longer beds his wife nor saying that he "admires" Maggie, and the play ending again with his chilling repetition of Big Daddy's earlier response to declarations of love, "Wouldn't it be funny it if that was true?"

Of all the many *Cats*, only this 1975 version and the "Cat Number One" text deserve serious attention, and as they have been successfully produced in recent years, there seems to be room enough for both. Individuals will differ as to preference according to whether they think the emphasis should be on Big Daddy's sense of tragedy or Maggie's qualified victory.

Personally, I prefer "Cat Number One," but Williams himself clearly approved of the American Shakespeare Company's production of this final version and requested its publication by New Directions.

Pace Aristotle, what matters most in *Cat* is not the plot but the coherence of its unforgettable characters and their strikingly individual styles of speech: the desperately gallant and eloquent Maggie the Cat, torn between self interest and longing vulnerability; Big Daddy, the no-nonsense planter, trying to face the ultimate denial of death with his customary blunt honesty; and immobilized and withdrawn between them, Brick, the self-destructive golden boy whose devotion to "Echo Spring" recalls the Greek myth of love irreparably lost but impossible to forget. It is these vivid characterizations that have won for *Cat* its place among the "big three" of Williams *oeuvre*, alongside *The Glass Menagerie* and *A Streetcar Named Desire*.

May 2004

Brian Parker is an Emeritus Professor of English at the University of Toronto, where he served as Director of the Graduate Drama Centre, Director of Graduate English Studies, and Dean of Arts and Vice-Provost of Trinity College. Since retirement, Parker's work on the Williams mss. has been supported by fellowships from the Fulbright Foundation, the Bibliographical Society of America, the Andrew Mellon Foundation (at the Humanities Research Center in Austin), and the Social Sciences and Humanities Research Council of Canada.

AUTHOR AND DIRECTOR:
A DELICATE SITUATION

by Tennessee Williams

Whether he likes it or not, a writer for the stage must face the fact that the making of a play is, finally, a collaborative venture, and plays have rarely achieved a full-scale success without being in some manner raised above their manuscript level by the brilliant gifts of actors, directors, designers, and frequently even the seasoned theatrical instincts of their producers. I often wonder, for personal instance, if *The Glass Menagerie* might not have been a mere *succès d'estime,* snobbishly remembered by a small coterie, if Laurette Taylor had not poured into it her startling light and power, or if, without the genius of Kazan, *A Streetcar Named Desire* could have been kept on the tracks in those dangerous, fast curves it made here and there, or if the same genius was not requisite to making *Cat on a Hot Tin Roof* acceptable to a theater public which is so squeamish about a naked study of life.

A playwright's attitude toward his fellow workers goes through a cycle of three main phases. When he is just beginning in his profession, he is submissive mostly out of intimidation, for he is "nobody" and almost everybody that he works with is "somebody." He is afraid to assert himself, even when demands are made on him which, complied with, might result in a distortion of his work. He will permit lines, speeches, sometimes even whole scenes to be cut from his script because a director has found them difficult to direct or an actor has found them difficult to act. He will put in or build up a scene for a star at the sacrifice of the play's just proportions and balance. A commercial producer can sometimes even bully him into softening the denouement of his play with the nearly always wrong idea that this will improve its chances at the box office. Or if he is suddenly driven to resistance, he is unable to offer it with a cool head and a tactful tongue. Intimidation having bottled him up until now, he now pops off with unnecessary violence, he flips his lid. That's the first phase of the cycle. The second is entered when the playwright has scored his first notable success. Then the dog has his day. From intimidation he passes into the opposite condition. All of a sudden he is the great, uncompromising Purist, feeling that all ideas but his own are threats to the integrity of his work. Being suddenly a "Name" playwright, explosions of fury are no longer necessary for him to get his way. Now that he has some weight, he throws it around with the assured nonchalance of a major league pitcher warming up by the dugout. When his script is submitted to a producer by his representatives, it is not unlike the bestowal of a crown in heaven, there is a sanctified solemnity and hush about the proceedings. The tacit implication is: Here it is; take it or leave it; it will not be altered, since the slightest alteration would be nearly as sacrilegious as a revision of the Holy Scriptures.

Some playwrights are arrested at this second phase of the cycle, which is really only an aggravated reaction to the first, but sometimes the inevitable eventuality of an important failure after an important success or series of successes, will result in a moderation of the playwright's embattled ego. The temple or citadel of totally unsullied self-expression has not proven as secure a refuge as it seemed to him when he first marched triumphantly into it. It may take only one failure, it may take two or three, to persuade him that his single assessment of his work is fallible, and meanwhile, if he is not hopelessly paranoiac, he has come to learn of the existence of vitally creative minds in other departments of theater than the writing department, and that they have much to offer him, in the interpretation, the clarification, and illumination of what he has to say; and even if, sometimes, they wish him to express, or let him help them express, certain ideas and feelings of their own, he has now recognized that there are elements of the incomplete in his nature and in the work it produces. This is the third phase. There is some danger in it. There is the danger that the playwright may be as abruptly divested of confidence in his own convictions as that confidence was first born in him. He may suddenly become a sort of ventriloquist's dummy for ideas which are not his own at all. But that is a danger to which only the hack writer is exposed, and so it doesn't much matter. A serious playwright can only profit from passage into the third phase, for what he will now do is this: he will listen; he will consider; he will give a receptive attention to any creative mind that he has the good fortune to work with. His own mind, and its tastes, will open like the gates of a city no longer under siege. He will then be willing to supplement his personal conceptions with outside conceptions which he will have learned may be creative extensions of his own.

A mature playwright who has made this third and final step in his relations to fellow workers has come to accept the collaborative nature of the theater: he knows now that each artist in the theater is able to surpass his personal limits by respect for and acceptance of the talent and vision of others. When a gifted young actor rushes up to the playwright during rehearsals and cries out, I can't feel this, this doesn't ring true to me, the writer doesn't put on the austere mask of final authority. He moves over another seat from the aisle of a rehearsal hall, and bows his head in serious reflection while the actor tells him just what about the speech or the scene offends his sense of artistic justice, and usually the writer gets something from it. If he still disagrees with the actor, he says: "Let's get together with (whoever is directing) and talk this over at the bar next door. . . ." Maybe he won't sleep that night, but the chances are that in the morning he will reexamine the challenged segment with a sympathetic concern for an attitude which hasn't originated in his own brain and nerves, where sensibility is seated.

Now all of this that I've been rambling on about is my idea of the healthy course of development for a playwright *except*— I repeat, EXCEPT!—in those rare instances when the playwright's work is so highly individual that no one but the playwright is capable of discovering the right key for it. When this rare instance occurs, the playwright has just two alternatives. Either he must stage his play himself or he must find one particular director who has the very unusual combination of a truly creative imagination plus a true longing, or even just a true willingness, to devote his own gifts to the faithful projection of someone else's vision. This is a thing of rarity. There are very few directors who are imaginative and yet also willing to forego the willful imposition of their own ideas on a play. How can you blame them? It is all but impossibly hard for any artist to devote his gifts to the mere interpretation of the gifts of another. He wants to leave his own special signature on whatever he works on.

Here we encounter the sadly familiar conflict between playwright and director. And just as a playwright must recognize the value of conceptions outside his own, a director of serious plays must learn to accept the fact that nobody knows a play better than the man who wrote it. The director must know that the playwright has already produced his play on the stage of his own imagination, and just as it is important for a playwright to forget certain vanities in the interest of the total creation of the stage, so must the director. I must observe that certain directors are somewhat too dedicated to the principle that all playwrights must be "corrected." I don't think a director should accept a directorial assignment without feeling that, basically, the author of the play, if it's a serious work by a playwright of ability, has earned and deserves the right to speak out, more or less freely, during the rehearsal and tryout period of the production if this can be done in a way that will not disturb the actors. Yet it sometimes happens that the playwright is made to feel a helpless bystander while his work is being prepared for Broadway. It seems to me that the director is privileged to tell the author to "Shut up!" actually or tacitly, only when it is unmistakably evident that he, the director, is in total artistic command of the situation. Sometimes a director will go immediately from one very challenging and exhausting play production into another, being already committed by contract to do so. Then naturally he can't bring the same vitality to the second that he brought to the first. This becomes evident when the play has been blocked out, and after this blocking, little further progress is being made. The play remains at the stage of its initial blocking. The director may say, and quite honestly feel, that what he is doing is giving the public and critics a play precisely as it was written. However, this is evading the need and obligation that I mentioned first in this article, that a play must nearly always be raised above its manuscript level by the creative gifts and energies of its director, and all others involved in its production.

Perhaps it would be a good idea, sometimes, to have a good psychiatrist in attendance at the rehearsals and tryout of a difficult play, one who is used to working with highly charged creative people such as directors and actors and playwrights and producers, so that whenever there is a collision of nervous, frightened, and defensive egos, he can arbitrate among them, analyze their personal problems which have caused their professional problems, and "smooth things over" through the clearing house of a wise and objective observer.

Once in a while the exigencies and pressures of Broadway must step aside for another set of conditions which are too fragile and spiritually important to suffer violence through the silly but sadly human conflict of egos.

The theater *can* be a maker of great friendships!

This essay first appeared in *Playbill,* September 30, 1957.

A CHRONOLOGY

1907   June 3: Cornelius Coffin Williams and Edwina Estelle Dakin marry in Columbus, Mississippi.

1909   November 19: Sister, Rose Isabelle Williams, is born in Columbus, Mississippi.

1911   March 26: Thomas Lanier Williams III is born in Columbus, Mississippi.

1918   July: Williams family moves to St. Louis, Missouri.

1919   February 21: Brother, Walter Dakin Williams, is born in St. Louis, Missouri.

1928   Short story "The Vengeance of Nitocris" is published in *Weird Tales* magazine.

   July: Williams' grandfather, Walter Edwin Dakin (1857-1954), takes young Tom on a tour of Europe.

1929   September: Begins classes at the University of Missouri at Columbia.

1930   Writes the one-act play *Beauty is the Word* for a local contest.

1932   Summer: Fails ROTC and is taken out of college by his father and put to work as a clerk at the International Shoe Company.

1936   January: Enrolls in extension courses at Washington University, St. Louis.

1937   March 18 and 20: First full-length play, *Candles to the*

Sun, is produced by the Mummers, a semi-professional theater company in St. Louis.

September: Transfers to the University of Iowa.

November 30 and December 4: *Fugitive Kind* is performed by the Mummers.

1938   Graduates from the University of Iowa with a degree in English.

Completes the play, *Not About Nightingales.*

1939   *Story* magazine publishes "The Field of Blue Children" with the first printed use of his professional name, "Tennessee Williams."

Receives an award from the Group Theatre for a group of short plays collectively titled *American Blues*, which leads to his association with Audrey Wood, his agent for the next thirty-two years.

1940   January through June: Studies playwriting with John Gassner at the New School for Social Research in New York City.

December 30: *Battle of Angels*, starring Miriam Hopkins, suffers a disastrous first night during its out-of-town tryout in Boston and closes shortly thereafter.

1942   December: At a cocktail party thrown by Lincoln Kirstein in New York, meets James Laughlin, founder of New Directions, who is to become Williams' lifelong friend and publisher.

1943   Drafts a screenplay, *The Gentleman Caller*, while under contract in Hollywood with Metro Goldwyn Mayer: rejected by the studio, he later rewrites it as *The Glass Menagerie*.

October 13: A collaboration with his friend Donald Windham, *You Touched Me!* (based on a story by D.H. Lawrence), premieres at the Cleveland Playhouse.

1944   December 26: *The Glass Menagerie* opens in Chicago starring Laurette Taylor.

A group of poems titled "The Summer Belvedere" is published in *Five Young American Poets, 1944*. (All books listed here are published by New Directions unless otherwise indicated.)

1945   March 25: *Stairs to the Roof* premieres at the Pasadena Playhouse in California.

March 31: *The Glass Menagerie* opens on Broadway and goes on to win the Drama Critics Circle Award for best play of the year.

September 25: *You Touched Me!* opens on Broadway, and is later published by Samuel French.

December: *27 Wagons Full of Cotton and Other Plays* is published.

1947   Summer: Meets Frank Merlo (1929-1963) in Provincetown—starting in 1948 they become lovers and companions, and remain together for fourteen years.

December 3: *A Streetcar Named Desire*, directed by Elia Kazan and starring Jessica Tandy, Marlon Brando, Kim Hunter and Karl Malden, opens on Broadway to rave reviews and wins the Pulitzer Prize and the Drama Critics Circle Award.

1948   October 6: *Summer and Smoke* opens on Broadway and closes in just over three months.

1949   January: *One Arm and Other Stories* is published.

1950   The novel *The Roman Spring of Mrs. Stone* is published.

The film version of *The Glass Menagerie* is released.

1951   February 3: *The Rose Tattoo* opens on Broadway starring Maureen Stapleton and Eli Wallach and wins the Tony Award for best play of the year.

The film version of *A Streetcar Named Desire* is released starring Vivian Leigh as Blanche and Marlon Brando as Stanley.

1952   April 24: A revival of *Summer and Smoke* directed by Jose Quintero and starring Geraldine Page opens off-Broadway at the Circle at the Square and is a critical success.

The National Institute of Arts and Letters inducts Williams as a member.

1953   March 19: *Camino Real* opens on Broadway and after a harsh critical reception closes within two months.

1954   A book of stories, *Hard Candy*, is published in August.

1955   March 24: *Cat on a Hot Tin Roof* opens on Broadway directed by Elia Kazan and starring Barbara Bel Geddes, Ben Gazzara and Burl Ives. *Cat* wins the Pulitzer Prize and the Drama Critics Circle Award.

The film version of *The Rose Tattoo*, for which Anna Magnani later wins an Academy Award, is released.

1956   The film *Baby Doll*, with a screenplay by Williams and directed by Elia Kazan, is released amid some controversy and is blacklisted by Catholic leader Cardinal Spellman.

June: *In the Winter of Cities*, Williams' first book of poetry, is published.

1957   March 21: *Orpheus Descending*, a revised version of *Battle of Angels*, directed by Harold Clurman, opens on Broadway but closes after two months.

1958   February 7: *Suddenly Last Summer* and *Something Unspoken* open off-Broadway under the collective title *Garden District*.

The film version of *Cat on a Hot Tin Roof* is released.

1959   March 10: *Sweet Bird of Youth* opens on Broadway and runs for three months.

The film version of *Suddenly Last Summer*, with a screenplay by Gore Vidal, is released.

1960   November 10: The comedy *Period of Adjustment* opens on Broadway and runs for over four months.

The film version of *Orpheus Descending* is released under the title *The Fugitive Kind*.

1961   December 29: *The Night of the Iguana* opens on Broadway and runs for nearly ten months.

The film versions of *Summer and Smoke* and *The Roman Spring of Mrs. Stone* are released.

1962   The film versions of *Sweet Bird of Youth* and *Period of Adjustment* are released.

1963   January 15: *The Milk Train Doesn't Stop Here Anymore* opens on Broadway, starring Tallulah Bankhead, and immediately closes due to a blizzard and a newspaper strike.

September: Frank Merlo dies of lung cancer.

1964   The film version of *Night of the Iguana* is released.

1966   February 22: *Slapstick Tragedy* (*The Mutilated* and *The Gnädiges Fräulein*) runs on Broadway for less than a week.

December: A novella and stories are published under the title *The Knightly Quest*.

1968   March 27: *Kingdom of Earth* opens on Broadway under the title *The Seven Descents of Myrtle*.

The film version of *The Milk Train Doesn't Stop Here Anymore* is released under the title *Boom!*

1969   May 11: *In the Bar of a Tokyo Hotel* opens off-Broadway and runs for three weeks.

Committed by his brother Dakin for three months to the Renard Psychiatric Division of Barnes Hospital in St. Louis.

The film version of *Kingdom of Earth* is released under the title *The Last of the Mobile Hot Shots*.

Awarded Doctor of Humanities degree by the University of Missouri and a Gold Medal for Drama by the American Academy of Arts and Letters.

1970   February: A book of plays, *Dragon Country,* is published.

1971   Williams breaks with his agent Audrey Wood. Bill Barnes assumes his representation, and then later Mitch Douglas.

1972   April 2: *Small Craft Warnings* opens off-Broadway.

   Williams is given a Doctor of Humanities degree by the University of Hartford.

1973   March 1: *Out Cry,* the revised version of *The Two-Character Play,* opens on Broadway.

1974   September: *Eight Mortal Ladies Possessed,* a book of short stories, is published.

   Williams is presented with an Entertainment Hall of Fame Award and a Medal of Honor for Literature from the National Arts Club.

1975   The novel *Moise and the World of Reason* is published by Simon and Schuster and Williams' *Memoirs* is published by Doubleday.

1976   January 20: *This Is (An Entertainment)* opens in San Francisco.

   June: *The Red Devil Battery Sign* closes during its out-of-town tryout in Boston.

   November 23: *Eccentricities of a Nightingale,* a rewritten version of *Summer and Smoke,* opens in New York.

   April: Williams' second volume of poetry, *Androgyne, Mon Amour,* is published.

1977   May 11: *Vieux Carrè* opens on Broadway and closes within two weeks.

1978   *Tiger Tail* premieres at the Alliance Theater in Atlanta, Georgia and a revised version premieres the following year at the Hippodrome Theater in Gainsville, Florida.

1979   January 10: *A Lovely Sunday for Creve Coeur* opens off-Broadway.

        Kirche, Kutchen, und Kinder premieres off-Broadway at the Jean Cocteau Repertory Theater.

        Williams is presented with a Lifetime Achievement Award at the Kennedy Center Honors in Washington by President Jimmy Carter.

1980   January 25: *Will Mr. Merriwether Return from Memphis?* premieres for a limited run at the Tennessee Williams Performing Arts Center in Key West, Florida.

        March 26: Williams' last Broadway play, *Clothes for a Summer Hotel*, opens and closes after 15 performances.

1981   August 24: *Something Cloudy, Something Clear* premieres off-Broadway at the Jean Cocteau Repertory Theater.

1982   May 8: The second of two versions of *A House Not Meant to Stand* opens for a limited run at the Goodman Theater in Chicago.

1983   February 24: Williams is found dead in his room at the Hotel Elysee in New York City. It is determined from an autopsy that the playwright died from asphyxiaton, choking on a plastic medicine cap.

Williams is later buried in St. Louis.

1984   July: *Stopped Rocking and Other Screenplays* is published.

1985   November: *Collected Stories,* with an introduction by Gore Vidal, is published."

1995   The first half of Lyle Leverich's important biography, *Tom: The Unknown Tennessee Williams* is published by Crown Publishers.

1996   September 5: Rose Isabelle Williams dies in Tarrytown, New York.

        September 5: *The Notebook of Trigorin,* in a version revised by Williams, opens at the Cincinnati Playhouse in the Park.

1998   March 5: *Not About Nightingales* premieres at the Royal National Theatre in London, directed by Trevor Nunn, later moves to Houston, Texas, and opens November 25, 1999 on Broadway.

1999   November: *Spring Storm* is published.

2000   May: *Stairs to the Roof* is published.

        November: *The Selected Letters of Tennessee Williams, Volume I* is published.

2001   June: *Fugitive Kind* is published.

2002   April: *Collected Poems* is published.

2004   August: *Candles to the Sun* is published.

        November: *The Selected Letters of Tennessee Williams, Volume II* is published.

PLAYWRIGHTS AND THEIR PLAYS
published by New Directions

Wolfgang Borchert
The Man Outside

Mikhail Bulgakov
Flight & Bliss

Jean Cocteau
The Infernal Machine & Other Plays

H.D.
Ion and *Hippolytus Temporizes*

Lawrence Ferlinghetti
Routines (experimental plays)

Goethe
Faust, Part I

Alfred Jarry
Ubu Roi

Heinrich von Kleist
Prince Friedrich of Homburg

P. Lal
Great Sanskrit Plays in Modern Translation

Federico García Lorca
Five Plays: Comedies and Tragicomedies
The Public and *Play Without a Title*
Three Tragedies:
The House of Bernard Alba
Blood Wedding
Yerma

Abby Mann
Judgment at Nuremberg

Michael McClure
Gorf

Carson McCullers
The Member of the Wedding

Henry Miller
Just Wild About Harry

Ezra Pound
The Classic Noh Theatre of Japan
Elektra
Women of Trachis

Kenneth Rexroth
Beyond the Mountains (four plays in verse)

Andrew Sinclair
Adventures in the Skin Trade
(based on the novel by Dylan Thomas)

Dylan Thomas
> *The Doctor and the Devils* (film and radio scripts)
> *Under Milk Wood*

Tennessee Williams
> *Baby Doll & Tiger Tail*
> **Battle of Angels*
> *Camino Real*
> *Candles to the Sun*
> *Cat on a Hot Tin Roof*
> *Clothes for a Summer Hotel*
> **The Eccentricities of a Nightingale*
> *Fugitive Kind*
> *The Glass Menagerie*
> **In the Bar of a Tokyo Hotel*
> **Kingdom of Earth*
> *A Lovely Sunday for Creve Coeur*
> **The Milk Train Doesn't Stop Here Anymore*
> **The Night of the Iguana*
> *Not About Nightingales*
> *The Notebook of Trigorin*
> **Orpheus Descending*
> **Period of Adjustment*
> **The Red Devil Battery Sign*
> **The Rose Tattoo*
> **Small Craft Warnings*
> *Something Cloudy, Something Clear*
> *Spring Storm*
> *Stairs to the Roof*
> *Stopped Rocking & Other Screenplays*
> *A Streetcar Named Desire*

Suddenly Last Summer
Summer and Smoke
Sweet Birth of Youth
27 Wagons Full of Cotton (one-act plays)
The Two-Character Play
Vieux Carré

*available in *Volumes 1* through 8 of *The Theatre of Tennessee Williams*

William Carlos Williams
Many Loves and Other Plays

PLEASE VISIT OUR WEBSITE

www.ndpublishing.com

OR ORDER FROM YOUR LOCAL BOOKSTORE